P9-CCO-561

738.5 MARSHALL
Marshall, Marlene Hurley
Making bits & pieces
   mosaics

Central

APR 0 7 1999

CENTRAL LIBRARY

Making
Bits & Pieces
MOSAICS

Creative Projects for Home & Garden

MARLENE HURLEY MARSHALL

PHOTOGRAPHY BY SABINE VOLLMER VON FALKEN

 STOREY BOOKS
Schoolhouse Road
Pownal, Vermont 05261

*The mission of Storey Communications is to serve our customers
by publishing practical information that encourages personal independence
in harmony with the environment.*

Edited by Deborah L. Balmuth
Art direction and design by Meredith Maker
Production by Meredith Maker and Erin Lincourt
Photography by Sabine Vollmer von Falken
Photograph on page 1 by the author; on pages 2, 29 courtesy of *Quirky Gardens,* Ten Speed Press, 1995;
on pages 3, 4, 5, 6, 7, 71 courtesy of Seymour Rosen, SPACES; on page 8 courtesy of Capital Children's Museum;
on pages 9, 53 by Lucille Krasne; on page 34 by Michael Doherty; on page 36 by Nicholas Whitman;
on pages 73, 86 by Katherine Matheson Kaplan, Relics; and on pages 84, 85 courtesy of the
Miami-Dade Transit Agency, photographer Bobbie C. Crichton.
Illustrations by Alison Kolesar
Indexed by Word•a•bil•i•ty

Copyright © 1998 by Marlene Hurley Marshall

All rights reserved. No part of this book may be reproduced without written permission from the publisher,
except by a reviewer who may quote brief passages or reproduce illustrations in a review with appropriate credits;
nor may any part of this book be reproduced, stored in a retrieval system, or transmitted in any form or by any means —
electronic, mechanical, photocopying, recording, or other — without written permission from the publisher.

The information in this book is true and complete to the best of our knowledge. All recommendations are made
without guarantee on the part of the author or Storey Communications, Inc. The author and publisher disclaim any liability
in connection with the use of this information.
For additional information please contact Storey Communications, Inc., Schoolhouse Road, Pownal, Vermont 05261.

Storey books are available for special premium and promotional uses and for customized editions.
For further information, please call the Custom Publishing Department at 1-800-793-9396.

Printed in Hong Kong by C & C Offset Printing Co., Ltd.
10 9 8 7 6 5 4 3 2 1

Library of Congress Cataloging-in-Publication Data

Marshall, Marlene Hurley.
    Making bits & pieces mosaics : creative projects for home & garden /
Marlene Hurley Marshall : photography by Sabine Vollmer von Falken.
        p.   cm.
    Includes index.
    ISBN 1-58017-015-3 (alk. paper)
    1. Mosaics—Technique. I. Title
TT910.M27 1998
738.5—dc21   97-31831
                                                                     CIP

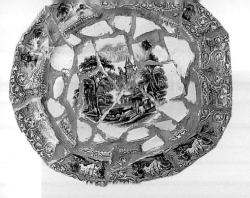

CONTENTS

DEDICATION

To the memory of my mother and father,

Alice Wilkinson and Daniel Hurley.

ACKNOWLEDGMENTS

Many thanks to my loving and supportive family for all their help and enthusiasm for this project. To my son, Michael Doherty, and his wife, Xanthi; and my daughters, Leigh and Marlo Doherty. Also my sister, Sheila Luciano, and her husband, Joe; my brothers, Daniel Hurley and his wife, Alice, Michael Hurley, and his wife, Marge.

My thanks to all my encouraging friends: Reginald Madison, Michele Cabrera, Val Fournier, Arline Reiley, Helen Thomas, Janet Cooper, and Sabine Vollmer von Falken for their assistance, resources, and suggestions.

I am grateful to Elizabeth Weber, Cindy Sherman, Jim and Chris Scrimgeour, Tracy Delsignore from Dry Goods, Robin Ban from Seeds, Carol Levinson from Once Upon a Table, Seymour Rosen from SPACES, Carol Schultze, and Penny Weinstein — all helped make this project possible.

To all the contributing artists past and present — Carlos Alves, Linda Benswanger, Nek Chand, Evelyn Ferrier, Antoni Gaudí, Albert Glade, Raymond Isidore, Katherine Matheson Kaplan, Jim Power, Tressa Prisbrey, Simon Rodia, Caroline Warwick — for their generous enthusiasm, information, and inspiration.

To my editor, Deborah Balmuth, for her gentle and keen suggestions to guide my way; Meredith Maker for her creative assistance; and Janet Lape for her attention to detail.

Last, to my grandson, Quinn James Doherty, for his inspiration.

PREFACE

I am fascinated by old china. It conjures remembrances of childhood, shared meals, and family life. Broken shards of china are artifacts of another time and place, a living history with great charm and allure.

My habit of collecting shards began with a discovery I made after moving to an old farmhouse in western Massachusetts. While turning the soil for flower beds, I unearthed pottery shards. Every day I dug, I found more. I could not bring myself to throw these shards away, so they began accumulating, and I placed them as a decorative touch on the topsoil of my houseplants.

I knew that my farmhouse was more than 150 years old, which made the pieces all the more enthralling. What stories did they carry with them, of meals and celebrations, food grown and cooked, and the accidents that led to their breakage?

Not long after, I began to notice decorative Victorian garden pots and small tables with china-encrusted surfaces at flea markets and antiques shops. I learned that this popular decorative technique was called by several names during the Victorian era: memoryware, bits and pieces, and putty pots. These pieces dazzled me — my love affair with this art form had begun. In a short time, I started to amass a collection of chipped dishes and began cementing together my own version of this captivating art: ancestral yet homey, dignified yet sort of kitschy.

More than a decade has passed since my first encounter with the garden shards and the Victorian putty pots, yet I'm still enchanted. I have made roomfuls of pieces from shards, from three-foot-high matching garden urns to tables, fireplace mantels, mirrors, and chairs. My collection of dishes multiplied from one box full to an entire studio full, and my obsession even led to the development of a wholesale business. When I reflect on this odyssey today, there is no one more surprised than I am about how these homey shards have directed my life's vocation to such a magnitude!

When I go to see any great house I inquire first for the china closet, and next for the picture gallery.

— Charles Lamp, 1832, English writer

Chapter One

INTRODUCTION TO
BITS & PIECES MOSAICS

This folk art has been known by many names at different times and in different cultures: bits and pieces, *pique assiette* (a French term that translates as "stolen from plate"), putty pots, and memoryware. The basic process draws on the techniques of traditional mosaics: gathered pieces of broken pottery, china, glass, buttons, figurines, and jewelry are cemented onto a base to create a new surface. Almost any form can be used as a base, and any combination of pieces can be applied, restricted only by the individual creator's imagination.

This craft is open to almost anyone, since the expense is minimal (most of the materials are recycled castoffs), and although it does require some attention to detail in color and arrangement, no particular artistic talent is needed. By bringing together bits and pieces that have had other lives, served other purposes, and been part of another whole before, contemporary crafters can use this distinctive technique to produce truly original creations with overtones of the past.

This balustrade bench designed by Antoni Gaudí is one of his most colorful and playful works. It is an outstanding example of his distinctive use of broken bits of rubble on curved surfaces to create a sense of movement.

FOLK ART AND CRAFT

Art is the manifestation of the undying soul of the people. It is the aspect of their genius which is manifest in the great work, no less in the day to day utensil which they used.

— Maya Angelou

Folk arts and crafts foster a sense of identity among people in a particular culture, both as individuals and as a society. Bits and pieces mosaics invite people to celebrate their place in a culture that has been passed down to them and continues on after them. The shards are reminders of the everyday activities of those who have lived before us and of what we have in common: a need to eat, to provide for our families, and to embellish our homes.

When I display my shardwork creations at craft or antiques shows, people of all ages are surprised and captivated by the fantasy, even mystery, contained in the pieces. In examining the simple shards, smiles break forth on people's faces, and these relative strangers tell me what they see in the pieces and ask

This garden wall, dating from 1855, was created by a Cornish woman, Caroline Warwich, in Ballarat, Victoria, Australia. It is thought that she was inspired by an old Celtic decorative custom of embellishing surfaces with shells and decorative kitchen pottery. Her garden is now a museum.

how I create them. They also want to touch these pieces, being drawn to the human element in the history of the shards.

There is a story behind every bit and piece: where it came from, how it got broken, how it got into the artist's hands, and its function and meaning in the lives of various people along the way. The shardwork sparks speculation and memories in observers, who are reminded of precious pieces of their own past.

Examples around the World

Shard art adorns both civic structures and private homes all over the world. In medieval Europe, this decorative technique was practiced by a group of Roman families called the Cosmati, a cooperative of stonemasons and sculptors who recycled marble fragments from ancient ruins and combined them with cubes of colored glass to produce intricate geometric patterns on new surfaces. They decorated everything from cloister columns to candleholders, with their splendid Cosmateque floors recognized as their masterpieces.

Many of the temples and ancient palaces of Vietnam are embellished with mosaics. In Hue, the former capital, gates of brick decorated with shards breach the wall of the Imperial Enclosure of the Emperor Gia Long, built in the early eighteenth century. In Thailand, fabulous examples can be seen in Bangkok at Wat Arun and the Palace Museum.

Antoni Gaudí

Spanish architect and designer Antoni Gaudí (1852–1926) introduced the bits and pieces technique to Spain when he designed the twisting balustrade bench for Parque Guell in Barcelona (photo on page 1). Originally envisioned as a garden city, the proposed sixty residences were never built, and the park became city property in 1923. It is one of Gaudí's most colorful and playful works, and an outstanding example of his distinctive use of curved surfaces to create a sense of movement. His extraordinary bench is atop a plaza overlooking the city and the sea. It is brightly decorated with pieces of broken glazed ceramics and bits of rubble called in Spanish *trencadis* (ceramic fragments).

Nek Chand Saini

In 1958, Nek Chand Saini began creating his Rock Garden on the outskirts of Chandigarh, India. Employed as a road inspector during the day, he worked on his sculptures at night. He transported the recycled material he used

THE FANTASY GARDEN

Indian artist Nek Chand worked with hundreds of enthusiastic schoolchildren in Washington, D.C., to build a permanent fantasy garden at the Capital Children's Museum. The museum's president, Ann Lewin, had visited Nek Chand's Rock Garden in India and felt "as if I were walking through a man's soul." A meeting with the artist generated the idea for the children's garden, the first of his work outside India. Fifty tons of sculpture from the artist's collection were shipped for free by the Indian government to the United States to create the garden. With the help of volunteers and children, Nek Chand designed the layout of the figures, animals, and fantasy objects that fill the museum's entranceway and courtyard.

for his art — boulders, scrap iron, and shards — to his deserted garden site on a bicycle. His twenty-five-acre garden contains near life-size sculptures covered with colorful smashed crockery and broken earthenware pots, slates, and tiles. Most of the walls enclosing the maze of walkways and courtyards are similarly covered in mosaics. The seventy-year-old artist continues to add to his creation, now a tourist attraction.

THE FATHER OF FRENCH
PIQUE ASSIETTE

Raymond Edouard Isidore, born in 1900 as the seventh of eight children in a poor French family, was a foundry worker and cemetery caretaker. An untutored artist motivated by a spiritual calling, Isidore began his life's work in 1938 by compulsively gathering bits of colored glass and pottery from the fields surrounding his house in Chartres, outside of Paris. "I was walking in the fields when I saw by chance bits of glass, porcelain debris, broken dishes," Isidore is reported to have said. "I gathered them, without a precise intention, for their colors and sparkle. The idea came to me to make with them a mosaic to decorate my house."

This wall, from the interior of Raymond Isidore's house, was one of the first surfaces the father of pique assiette *covered.*

Isidore devoted the rest of his life to covering every surface inside the house with bits and pieces, including all the furniture, down to the stove, stovepipe, clock, and even his wife's sewing machine. Next, he began work on the outside of the house and the small entrance courtyard. Then, he turned to the garden. He supplemented his field discoveries with things acquired at auctions, in quarries, and at the public dump. Because he used discarded bits of glass and broken dishes, his neighbors mocked him with the name *Picassiette,* which loosely translates as "plate stealer." They thought he was crazy and called him a sponger or leach. This did not discourage Isidore; he continued his work.

Most accounts of Isidore's life portray him as a misfit, a private, maniacal ornamentor. The term *picassiette,* which began as a derogatory term in reference to Isidore specifically, has been recast as a general term referring to the technique, and the words *pique assiette* are now used by many contemporary artists to refer to their work in this medium.

Isidore's house, Maison Picassiette, is a testament to the persistent force of creativity and a monument to its maker, a most uncommon man. Today it is a popular tourist attraction.

WATTS TOWERS

The Watts Towers stand as a monument to renewal and creativity arising out of urban waste; they are an urban salvage yard. The bases of the towers were formed of bent bar metal that was wrapped by hand with wire. The wire was then covered with cement into which the creator, Simon Rodia, embedded pieces of glass and seashells. All the materials used to create these towers were recycled, and the gathering of them became a community project undertaken by adults and children working together.

FRENCH FOLLOWERS

Robert Vasseur's inspiration to create *pique assiette* began in 1952 quite literally by accident, when he broke a dish. Since then he has been transforming his home in Louviers, France, into La Maison à Vasselle Cassée, patiently covering the entire house — inside and out — with rubble and dishes he collected at the public dump. Nothing has gone untouched, not even the doghouse. Like Isidore's, this house has become a tourist attraction.

SHARD ART IN THE UNITED STATES

This folk art flourished in the United States during the Victorian era, when it was referred to as bits and pieces, memoryware, putty pots, or shardware. The popular technique at this time involved applying wax or putty over glass, pottery, or furniture and then embedding shells, glass, small trinkets, porcelain figures, and other memorabilia into the soft surface before it hardened (photo on page vi). The finished surface of the putty was sometimes painted gold. The pieces of china (such as surviving tea sets) found on these Victorian pieces are antiques in their own right; the finished pieces are collector's items as well. The motifs of these pieces are a great resource for studying decorative domestic history and serve as a window into the past.

MONUMENTS BUILT BY AND FOR THE PEOPLE

There are a number of architectural monuments formed from recycled shard art. The most famous site is Watts Towers in Los Angeles, which Simon Rodia began constructing in 1921. This is yet another example of how this unique folk art has served as a creative outlet for the "common folk" in cultures throughout history, a voice for expressing the human spirit.

Albert Glade, a German immigrant and silent film actor of the 1920s, was another California artist inspired by recycled shards and materials. He spent ten years building his Enchanted Garden on the grounds of his Los Angeles home, by covering walkways and walls with bits of ceramics and shiny objects. Glade built four gardens during his lifetime; unfortunately, none of his work remains today. Glade's gardens were destroyed when his house was torn down soon after his death.

John Guidici was also intrigued by the process of embedding shards and bits of "this and that" in concrete. His odyssey into this medium began at the age of forty, when his son fell into his backyard pond and almost drowned. Guidici filled the pond with cement, and while it was still wet he pushed stones, colored glass, and figurines into the surface. Soon friends and neighbors were bringing him things to add to his creation, and Guidici found himself collecting pieces as well. Thus began fifty years of adding onto his whimsical garden. When asked at the age of ninety why he created his garden he replied, "Some people like to go to bars and drink. I like to play with cement."

Part of what makes this American decorative folk tradition so interesting is the layers of meaning that the many stray bits and pieces lend to the final product. The Wisconsin Concrete Park was created in 1948 by Fred Smith, an untutored folk artist. The park contains Smith's life-size figures of oxen and popular heroes, the surfaces of which are embedded with bits of glass and broken tiles. Besides being a monument to the hero depicted, each sculpture is imbued with other seemingly unrelated memories and sentiments that are carried by the bits and pieces, each a chronicle of its own past.

The act of embedding this material in concrete can be interpreted as an almost ritualistic act, giving the figure a past which presumably sustains it into the future.

— Michael Hall, *Reflection of American Fine and Folk Art*

Albert Glade's Enchanted Garden contained everything from old buttons to kitchen crockery and plastic dolls.

SHARD ART IN OUR OWN TIME

This shard child from Nek Chand Saini's Rock Garden is itself a "bit and piece" of a larger work. The artist captured scenes of Indian custom, everything from a mountain village to the kingdom of heaven.

In recent years, there has been mounting interest in this art form among artists and collectors alike. Designers, artists, and architects are using recycled shards to create new surfaces on the exteriors and interiors of homes, restaurants, and businesses around the world. There are also many small businesses devoted to creating gift items, tables, birdbaths, birdhouses, and mirrors for sale in retail stores nationwide. A new generation is creating, recycling, and preserving objects from our own time, using this ancient craft tradition.

CREATING YOUR OWN WORK

The works described in this chapter were created over many generations, reflecting many cultures. I hope that their universal kinship inspires you to create expressions of our own times and experiences.

In this book, I will teach you how to use this folk-art technique to create your own pieces. I have included examples of both my own work and the work of others, past and present, with the expectation that you will seek out your own inspiration. The great thing about this folk art is that no two pieces are ever the same. My hope is that you will discover the joy of collecting your treasures and creating a new life for them. You can also feel good about the practical benefits of practicing this craft — you're recycling pieces that would otherwise end up in landfills. This is always a great explanation to offer anyone who doesn't understand your obsession with this craft, which, as history attests to, can become very addictive.

After all the years I've spent surrounded by these splendid finishes and mounds of shards filled with color, I still delight in the collage of fragments — whether it is an antique Victorian piece I have just discovered, or some new project I have completed for my garden. My existence has been enriched by these simple broken pieces. This work has led to encounters with people of all types and ages who share a common interest in everyday china, and an appreciation of the way simple shards connect us to the lives of our ancestors.

THE MOSAIC MAN

JIM POWER is a mosaic artist who has literally brought the art of *pique assiette* to the streets of New York City. In 1988, Jim dedicated himself to brightening up Saint Mark's Place, a street in lower Manhattan, between Avenue A and Lafayette Street. Working with volunteers, Jim decorated the bases of lampposts and parking meters, and filled the cracks in the sidewalks with pieces of broken mirror, china, bottles, and bits of costume jewelry.

"If a person feels good for a minute when they notice a colorful, glimmering crack in the sidewalk as they pass, then that's what it is all about," says Jim. Over the course of five years, Jim and his assistants have constructed a "mosaic trail" that is about two miles long and includes eighty light posts. His most impressive project is a bits and pieces wall two stories high on the corner of Saint Mark's Place and Avenue A.

Jim's mosaic work can also be seen on the exteriors of several restaurants in New York, including such eateries as the Coffee Shop, The Scrap Bin, Alcatraz, and the Megador. In addition to his public "street work," Jim creates bits and pieces designs for more traditional artifacts, such as huge garden urns.

Chapter Two

COLLECTING AND DESIGNING WITH BITS & PIECES

O ne of the most creative parts of this technique is choosing your materials. The options are wide open, from bits and pieces of dishes, china figurines, buttons, glass, and jewelry to marbles and stray pieces of "this and that" that come your way. Each object you select carries with it a human story of the people who used and held it. Collecting bits and pieces is one of the most enjoyable ways to recycle for the present while connecting with the past. And as you apply your own creative energy to bringing together these pieces, yet another story begins with your unique form and vision.

With my interest in and fascination with working in this art form, bits and pieces seem to dance into my hands; my accumulation of shards happened without much effort. My inability to throw anything away also helped make me an enthusiastic fan of this technique. You'll be surprised at how quickly your collection grows. Just spread the word that you're searching for bits and pieces and the tools of your craft will find you.

I find my collection of shardware both intriguing and mysterious. There is a sense of a whole personality embodied in an object that is both beautiful and homely at the same time.

— Cheryl Katz, designer

BITS AND PIECES TO COLLECT

This decorative art can accommodate a great array of objects besides china. Here are some other things to look for:

- Crystal bottle stoppers
- Porcelain flowers
- Teapots
- Covers from sugar bowls, soup tureens, and casserole dishes
- Cups and saucers
- Dinner plates
- Candy dishes
- Seashells
- Marbles
- Tiles
- Junk jewelry
- Buttons
- Lids
- Drawer pulls
- Glass
- Mirrors
- Figurines
- Coins
- Ceramic knickknacks

The impulse to collect has roots deep in the human psyche. The botanical garden containing plants from around the world and the knickknack cupboard of a middle-class home share the same goal: to bring together pieces from many different sources to form a collection. Historian John Dixon Hunt observes that natural history collections originated as "a memory theatre of that complete world lost with Eden but recoverable by human skill." Botanical gardens, menageries, and mineral collections were all efforts to bring the scattered pieces of creation back together. A similar impulse to reconnect stimulates the mind of the bits and pieces mosaic artisan.

Once you start looking, you'll be amazed at the places you will find china shards. You'll stop for tag sales, yard sales, and flea markets with a newfound purpose, and you won't be as upset when a favorite dish crashes to the floor, since it will no longer be destined for the garbage can.

BEGIN AT HOME

You will most certainly find sufficient materials to begin a project just from everyday mishaps in your own household. Get your friends and neighbors in on the act as well by asking them to save their accidents and castaways. I've found that most people are dedicated savers because they do not like to see good things go to waste, and they will welcome the chance to clear out their odds and ends. A dealer in vintage china called me once because she had a box of plates that had arrived broken. She said, "It would make me feel better to see these wonderful pieces recycled into something meaningful that someone could enjoy." I have even come home to find boxes of china on my porch; I often never find out who the donor is, but their shards have yielded treasures.

FREQUENT FLEA MARKETS, THRIFT STORES, AND TAG SALES

No matter what part of the country you live in, there will always be a flea market, a thrift shop, or, depending on the weather and time of year, a good selection of yard and tag sales where you can go hunting for materials for your work. Keep your eyes open for a single chipped dish, a box full of broken dishes, tins of old buttons, or some wonderful costume jewelry. If you buy in multiples, then you'll have enough to design borders for large pieces.

If you really want to amass a large collection of dishes for your palette, put together a flyer and pass it out to dealers of fine china and porcelain to let them know that you are interested in using breakage for art projects. Some dealers may want to charge a small fee for their broken dreams; others will give the shards to you for free.

EXPLORE BEACHES AND ABANDONED OCEAN DUMP SITES

Beaches have always been a source of shells and pieces of worn bottle glass. Before laws were passed to prevent environmental damage, the ocean was used as a dump site. Now discarded bits of china, glass, and metal wash up along the coastline. You can seek out added treasures by locating the old dump sites. Ask at a local marina and someone is sure to assist in your treasure hunt. My friend Sally, who has explored a number of these sites, asserts that the best-preserved objects are found in shoreline spots that have been protected by outer islands. My cousin Jack recently discovered the same is true in Hong Kong. This type of treasure hunt can be an enjoyable addition to any summer vacation.

You will soon discover, if you have not already, that collecting is in itself an enjoyable pastime. It can take place all over the world or right in your own backyard. You will surely find your own sources of bits and pieces, china, and other shiny objects. The more dishes and sculptural elements you amass, the more colors and patterns you will have to choose from to enhance your projects.

DESIGNING WITH SHARDS

There are many moods and looks that can be achieved with this colorful medium. The great thing about the technique is that very little is set in stone. The mastic used to attach shards to the base takes eight hours to dry, so apply shards without worry. If you don't like the design that is emerging, just take them off and start on something new. Don't be afraid to experiment.

DEVELOPING A COLOR SCHEME

The first factor to consider in developing a design is the base you plan to use. The shape or style of the base, along with your choice of china, will influence your design. Once you've selected a shape, begin experimenting with placement, trying a few juxtapositions of color before choosing a color scheme. You'll find it best to have a range of shard colors to pick from at this initial planning stage, but a restricted palette can be a challenge to the imagination.

Think of the shards as paint chips. You can choose to make your color pathways random, or to create a solid color line. For a dramatic look, try surrounding

One of the most famous flea markets is the Brimfield Antique and Flea Market in the town of Brimfield in western Massachusetts. It is held only three times each year, usually in May, July, and September, for a full week each time. (Check with an antiques journal for the exact dates and times.) Dealers and buyers come to this market from all over the world. If you're looking for vast amounts of all kinds of merchandise, some wildly expensive, some near giveaways, this is an outrageously wonderful market. It is a place to find every piece of china imaginable, and many great buys. You will probably find some of the original antique Victorian shardwork here as well, although there seems to be less available for sale each year.

Be sure to dress comfortably, and wear very comfortable shoes because you will do a lot of walking. If you are coming a great distance, make hotel reservations far in advance.

Design several geometric bands of color to make a bold and striking look. By using strong, contrasting colors, you can accentuate the linear element of your design.

Run a ribbonlike form around the piece, which can start at the very top and continue all around to the base. You can create a delightful sense of movement with this design.

a solid band of color with all-white china shards or creating a swirling ribbon of solid color running down and around the piece. If you plan out your design in advance, you can mark off the sections on the base that will not be covered by white shards and then fill these in with color.

Color schemes are definitely a personal decision. Observe what color combinations catch your eye or match your decor, then collect similar-colored pieces of china so you can re-create the same combinations on your bits and pieces objects.

MATCHING THE SHAPES

It is helpful to have a good array of edge pieces from plates to apply around the edge of your base. Plate edges that are particularly colorful or feature unusual designs, strong patterns, or floral motifs make a good border on a garden pot or around the edge of a table. Edging your base with plate edge pieces can be a good way to get your design started. Many shards from one particular plate pattern can create a very pleasing design, and finding multiples from one design is helpful for creating borders. The smooth edges also give the piece a nice finished look. Since shards from different sources (cups, plates, figurines) have many different curves, some concave and some convex, it is worth taking some time to see if you can match the shape of the shard with the shape of the base where it will be applied. Using smaller pieces of shards also helps to fit around the curves.

ADDING HIGHLIGHTS

You might choose to design your piece around a dramatic sculptural highlight such as a piece of dangling jewelry, a mirror, a cup handle, or a three-dimensional piece of porcelain fruit. I often begin by selecting a sculptural element that inspires me, then set about finding china that complements its colors. The colors don't always have to be exact matches; try finding complementary colors, such as light greens for a grouping of pink and yellow flowers.

Another way to create highlights in your pieces is with color patterns. I sometimes use a patchwork-quilt-like pattern, placing pieces of a strong color such as orange strategically every five inches or so across the surface, and then filling in around these. The strong accent color pops out and makes the surface appear to dance before your eyes.

Another way to add highlights to your design is to place flower shapes strategically around the base and fill in the rest of the design with shards afterward.

IMPROVISING

Remember that this is more of an improvisational art form than most. Your own sense of fantasy and fun feeds the experience and shows through in the end creation. There are no hard-and-fast rules to creating a design in this medium; the rules come from your own tastes, preferences, and leaps of imagination. There is a freedom in creating a surface application knowing that almost any material can be incorporated. Delight in free play of creation with the expressive qualities that the materials offer in this art form. Once you have settled on the materials and the base you want to cover, you can make the finished design as open ended or as preplanned as you wish. The results are so immediately rewarding that you may just decide to let each piece develop as you go.

SOURCES OF INSPIRATION

Many designs arise out of the desire to save objects that have sentimental or artistic value but are no longer useful. Since this is truly a craft with an added level of expression — the stories the shards carry — the sources of inspiration are as varied as the shards themselves. Two sisters from Boston who inherited a set of six Bavarian teacups from their grandmother came to me after seeing my shardwork at a show. They felt that the collection of beautiful cups and saucers, divided between the two of them, would just gather dust in their homes and

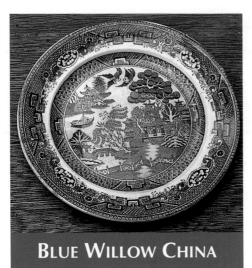

BLUE WILLOW CHINA

The romance of Blue Willow china has wooed popular taste for two centuries. The design depicts the legend of a Chinese maiden who is imprisoned for refusing to marry the elderly duke she is betrothed to. She and the man she loves escape and live happily for a time, but the spurned duke finds and kills them. The gods then raise the lovers to immortality in the form of two lovebirds.

Despite its Asian motif, the pattern originated in 1790 with an English manufacturer, the Spode Company, that designed it to be used as everyday china. Since there were no copyright laws in England at the time, the original design has been copied by more than 100 other manufacturers around the world. In America, the first manufacturer of Blue Willow was Buffalo Pottery in 1905. Prices of surviving pieces vary depending on their age and condition, the manufacturer, and the quality of the printing.

eventually get broken anyway. So I set to work smashing these lovely objects and used the shards to create new surfaces on a serving tray and a large vase. The finished pieces were ones that both sisters could use and enjoy in their daily lives, and still pass on to another generation as family heirlooms.

LEARNING BITS & PIECES ABOUT YOUR COLLECTION'S HISTORY

The patterns on china are keys to a culture and clues to a people. They reveal the everyday life of people: the patterns, designs, shapes, and colors they saw in the world, and the symbols and stories they valued and chose to portray on objects they looked at day after day. Shards of china are bits of living archaeology, the soul of a culture.

The wonderful thing about this craft is that you can use anything, but you may find, as I do, that you want to know more about the pieces you're collecting. There are many different types of china, glazes, and patterns. Each has its own unique composition of clay prepared and glazed in different ways, and fired at a specific temperature. You can explore the story of these styles by consulting a book on ceramic styles (see reading list on page 87). The histories behind the designs are often fascinating.

In addition to the story of how the shard itself was made, there is the story of the artist who glazed or designed the style and pattern of the piece. These range from centuries-old styles such as Chinese Blue and White to designs by twentieth-century artists such as Eva Zeisel.

CHINESE BLUE AND WHITE

This style, with a color scheme that has universal appeal, comes in a variety of patterns. One of the most popular of these patterns is Blue Willow, possibly the best-selling china pattern ever produced. The story behind this pattern (see box at left) captures the charm and romanticism of another time and place, and pays homage to a universal tale of enduring love.

During the reign of Chinese emperor Kangxi (1662–1722), blue-and-white porcelain was not popular in the imperial palace; the ruler favored ceramics in plain red, white, or blue. But the kilns never stopped producing blue-and-white vases, boxes, and dishes, primarily for export, and the porcelain became renowned throughout the Western world.

ZEISEL DINNERWARE

She may not be a household name, but Eva Zeisel's cups, bowls, dishes, and vases are scattered among the kitchen cabinets of the world. "Beauty cannot exist without someone to enjoy it," explains Zeisel, who pioneered the notion that the most humdrum household items also could be works of art.

In 1946, Eva Zeisel's avant-garde designs earned her a one-woman show at the Museum of Modern Art at the same time they were being offered in the Sears catalog. Her 1950s Hallcraft china design was touted as "America's fastest selling dinnerware." Forty-three years later, her designs are contemporary, fresh, captivating, and whimsical. A retrospective exhibit of her work was organized by the Smithsonian Institution in conjunction with the Musée des Arts Décoratifs in Montreal. In 1992, Ms. Zeisel was awarded the Brooklyn Museum's Lifetime Achievement Award. Her designs are in the permanent collection of most major art museums, as well as on the tables of a new generation of admirers. In 1992, at age eighty-five, Ms. Zeisel created a new line of Palazzetti designer furniture.

INSPIRATIONS OF THE CREATORS

Like Zeisel, Englishman Andrew Mellon was inspired by a love of china. He began his American career as an executive chef whose duties included buying the dishes for the corporate dining room where he worked. He later started a store where he sold discounted name-brand china. To indulge his interest in china and shards, Mellon teamed up with a china manufacturer, the Spode Company, and Mozayiks, a bits and pieces mosaic business based in Germantown, New York, to produce a natty collection of frames, planters, vases, and tabletops from Spode's broken and chipped earthenware.

As with many forms of art, bits and pieces mosaic can also have a therapeutic effect on those who undertake it. This is particularly poignant in situations where there has been devastating destruction that has literally broken things apart. Following the earthquake that shook the Simi Valley in California on January 17, 1994, two artists from the Ojai Valley volunteered to create a mosaic name-sign for the Katherine School with broken mementos. Working with students, families, and faculty from the school, Amy Mattison and Kim Hultgen used broken mementos from the lives affected by the quake to create a twelve-foot-long sign for the school.

We feel differently, more intimately, about dishes than we do about shoes or chairs or forks. If we unexpectedly come upon a chair like we used when we were children we say, 'We had a chair like that at home.' But if we come upon some dishes like we used on the dinner table with our parents we surely exclaim, 'Look! Our dishes!'

— Eva Zeisel, industrial designer,
On Being a Designer

Chapter Three

GETTING STARTED: THE BASIC TECHNIQUE

T he first wonderful thing about the bits and pieces technique is that it requires no special tools and very little investment in materials. The most useful tools can be found around the house, and if you don't have a specific tool, you can often improvise. If you've ever laid tile, you're likely to have the basic materials needed: glue, mastic, and unsanded grout. If not, you can purchase these at any hardware store. The only other supply you need is the shards themselves.

The second wonderful thing about this art form is that it doesn't require much practice or training before you are ready to begin your first project. In fact, the best way to learn is simply to dive in — pick a base, find a work space, gather the basic supplies and materials, and start assembling. You'll probably want to start small so you can experience the joy of completing a project fairly quickly, but the basic technique is the same, whether you're covering a tray top or a garden wall.

To begin is half the work.

— Ausonius

EQUIPMENT

Many of the commonly used tools and supplies are listed here, but do not let this limit your creative instincts. You may think of other pieces of equipment that will help in the process. My most cherished tools always end up being my hands.

◆ **Safety goggles.** It is absolutely essential to wear goggles when you are breaking shards.

◆ **Dust mask.** A mask should be worn when mixing grout, grinding edges, and sanding finished pieces.

◆ **Hammer.** A good strong hammer is needed for breaking dishes.

◆ **Wooden block or cutting board.** This provides a base surface for breaking dishes.

◆ **Heavy piece of canvas.** You may want to wrap dishes in canvas before breaking them with a hammer.

◆ **Whisk broom.** The small particles of broken shards can be used to fill small spaces.

◆ **Tile nippers.** These are excellent for selectively breaking pieces away from a center piece you want to preserve, or for cutting edge pieces.

◆ **Glass cutter.** If you are working with vintage glass, this is a useful tool for cutting clean-edged pieces.

◆ **Dremel.** This is not necessary when working with shards, but is helpful and very versatile. A Dremel is a small drill with interchangeable bits for buffing and grinding different surfaces. Note that grinding the edges on a high speed may chip the glaze on the china.

◆ **Ceramic tile metal file.** This tool is an alternative to a Dremel; it takes longer to accomplish the same degree of smoothness, but it works. I have also used a brick to smooth rough edges.

◆ **Coarse sandpaper.** Sand all base surfaces before you begin applying shards, and sand the sharp edges of shards on your finished piece.

◆ **Rubber gloves.** Wear heavy rubber gloves when applying grout, which is very drying to your skin.

◆ **Invisible glove cream.** This hand protectant is available at hardware stores, in either an aerosol can or a tube.

◆ **Bucket.** Keep a bucket full of clean water nearby as you work so you can rinse your hands periodically.

◆ **Jumbo craft sticks.** These are handy for applying mastic, making supports for heavy pieces while they're drying, and mixing and scraping off excess grout. They're available in craft stores.

◆ **Paring knife.** An old knife will work well for scraping off excess grout.

◆ **Terry towel.** You'll need a supply of clean, dry terry towels for lifting grout off your finished piece.

◆ **Spray bottle.** Keep a spray mister bottle of water nearby to moisten drying grout as you work.

◆ **Vinegar.** Rinsing your hands in vinegar when you are finished grouting will restore the pH balance of your skin.

◆ **Lazy Susan.** This revolving tray is a practical way to work on all sides of your piece without having to move it, and to design with a good overall view of your piece. It also helps minimize the need to handle the pieces during delicate stages of creation, and allows glue or grout to dry evenly. Lazy Susans come in many sizes to accommodate some very large pieces; both plastic and wooden models are available in kitchen supply and hardware stores.

◆ **Plastic containers.** Plastic containers make the best mixing bowls for grout and can be cleaned and reused easily. Allow leftover grout to dry overnight in the container and you will be able to pop it out and neatly dispose of it the next day.

MATERIALS

Besides shards and a base, the materials needed for a bits and pieces mosaic project are minimal. All of these products can be found in a hardware or tile store.

◆ **Mastic.** This adhesive for ceramic tile forms a strong bond on most surfaces and is perfect to use for the initial gluing of the shards and other bits of this and that. It is easily cleaned up with water while it is still wet, but you will need a solvent or scraper to remove it when completely dry, which takes about eight hours.

You can also get a clear, industrial-strength adhesive and sealant to attach heavier sculptural objects. This has a much faster drying time than mastic (approximately ten minutes) but it is very costly; I would only recommend it for selected pieces of a project.

Another substance I have used to hold some large elements is Bondo, a filler for dents on car surfaces. It gives larger pieces a permanent hold and makes a piece a solid mass. Bondo dries in seconds, so you must work quickly. It is also toxic, so follow the directions carefully.

◆ **Unsanded grout.** There are two kinds of grout: sanded, which is used for attaching tiles to floors, and unsanded, which is finer in texture and better for mosaic projects because it will not scratch china. Unsanded grout is sold in dry powdered form, which needs to be mixed with water or an acrylic additive before use. A pre-mixed grout is also on the market, but I don't recommend it because you cannot control its consistency. Unsanded grout is available in many colors.

Please note that all grout contains portland cement and silica sand. Reports on silica indicate that it may be a carcinogen, so always wear a mask when mixing grout. Heavy rubber gloves help protect your skin against the highly drying effects of grout.

◆ **Acrylic additive.** This is more expensive than the other materials listed here, but it is a strong hardener that you use in place of water when mixing grout. I recommend it for any project that will be exposed to moisture, such as a garden pot or a backsplash above a sink. It helps protect the piece from water damage, which can loosen the grout over time.

◆ **Grout pigments.** Colored pigments for grout come in almost every imaginable color. They usually can be purchased wherever grout is sold, and the cost is minimal. If you are working on a large project that requires a lot of grout, thoroughly combine the pigment with a large amount of dry unsanded grout to achieve a consistent color. Then mix just a small working amount of colored grout with water or acrylic additive.

SETTING UP YOUR WORK SPACE

Art is not what we are told it is

but what we discover or create:

art is an impulse, an instinct, and

our birthright: neither masterpiece

nor marble but gestures of the

spirit in a void forming the

characters and symbols

of a language of life itself.

— Beth Coffet, *In Celebration of Ourselves*

Most of your tools and your work space for this craft can be improvised. I spent an entire winter working on a large project right at my kitchen table. It wasn't ideal, but it's possible. As you look over the list of suggested equipment, don't be discouraged if you don't have or can't afford to buy some of these things. Think creatively, reuse, recycle — that's what this medium is all about!

While you can do this craft practically anywhere, it is highly desirable to have a permanent work space where you can leave projects in progress until they are completed. Shelves are useful for keeping all your tools and supplies close at hand. Space to store shards and bits of this and that in shoe boxes or similar containers will make it easier to choose the pieces you might need and keep the visual stimulation of the shards nearby.

It's very important to have a good worktable that allows you to work with the piece at eye level. You can elevate a piece with plastic milk crates or sturdy wooden boxes. You can also experiment with stools to find one that provides a comfortable working position.

The ideal floor and table surfaces are ones that can be easily swept after each project is completed. It is harder to work freely if you are worrying about keeping your work area clean or not dropping things on the floor. If you want to preserve the tabletop or floor, cover it with a large canvas or plastic drop cloth; this will take a lot of abuse and can be cleaned easily.

There are many ways to adjust the height of the piece you are working on: Use boxes to raise the piece to eye level, or, if the piece itself is very high, sit on a tall stool to put yourself in a better working position.

Selecting and Preparing a Base

Almost anything can be used as a base for your mastic. Old or recycled base pieces work just fine, since you're going to cover the surface. Just be sure that the structure is sturdy. You can easily learn to work around various shapes just by experimenting. The main challenge is to select shards that match the shape of your base.

Porous and Nonporous Surfaces

Bits and pieces mosaics can be created on almost any surface — wood, metal, terra-cotta, plastic. The only surface I've found that doesn't work is wood chip particleboard, which absorbs water and prevents the mastic from sticking. Materials that are porous, like terra-cotta or raw wood, are ideal because the mastic and the grout will adhere strongly to the surface, but I have worked on nonporous materials such as Formica. To condition these materials, drill holes all over the surface to give the mastic and grout places to adhere.

If your finished pieces will be exposed to moisture on a regular basis, you do not want an absorbant base. For works on an outdoor table or birdbath, a shower stall, or a backsplash over a sink, the base should be waterproof so that it does not absorb moisture and cause the mastic to fail. You will need to score the surface before applying mastic (as described in the backsplash project on page 49). Once you've finished applying the shards, paint the grout with a coat of clear water sealant to create a stronger moisture barrier. You should also be careful as you work to fill in the grout completely since any small hole will allow moisture in, which will break down the bond over time.

Preparing the Surface

Before you begin gluing on shards, it's essential to properly prepare the base. Make sure the overall structure of the base is strong. Check frames and furniture carefully and do any needed repairs or reinforcing before you begin. You do not want to apply all the shards onto a base only to have it fall apart. You should also clean the surface thoroughly to remove any dirt or grease, which can prevent the mastic from holding properly.

Some base surfaces require more preparation than others. Wooden surfaces with flaking paint chips need to be sanded lightly. Any nonporous surface, even ceramic, should be sanded or scored to create a better bond with the mastic and grout. A thin layer of mastic also will texturize the surface for better grip.

POSSIBLE BASE SURFACES

Lamp
Terra-cotta pot
Picture frame
Chair back
Mirror frame
Serving tray
Birdbath
Bathroom wall
Tabletop
Umbrella stand
Garden stones
Birdhouse
Wooden boxes and bowls
Wooden posts

I have even heard of someone who covered a microwave!

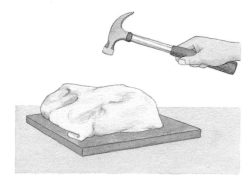

If you're not trying to salvage a particular design element in breaking a piece, wrap the plate or cup in canvas. You'll protect yourself from spattering shards. ▼

To salvage a plate's center design as a whole, turn the plate upsidedown and tap gingerly along its edge with a hammer. ▼

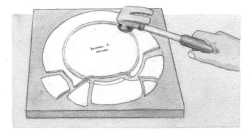

Use tile nippers to have more control over the break around a design element. You're more likely to salvage the center of a plate, for example, with this method. ▼

BREAKING SHARDS

You must always wear protective goggles when breaking dishes or any other type of ceramic piece. Relax before you strike. Remember, this is not an exact science; breaking shards is not like cutting out paper silhouettes with a fine-tipped pair of scissors. Not everything is going to break just as you would like it to, but there are a few things you can do to make it come close. Before beginning, determine which parts of the piece you want to use, and whether there are any pieces you want to try to isolate and preserve as a whole, such as a teapot spout, a cup handle, or a central design on a plate.

Random breaking. If you don't particularly care how the dish breaks, wrap it in a heavy piece of canvas and place it on a heavy wooden block. Hit it with a hammer several times, then open the canvas and check to see how your shards emerge. You may decide to hit them some more or use them as they are.

Controlled breaking. If there are particular pieces you want to preserve, keep the dish uncovered as you hit so you see exactly where you are breaking, giving you a little more control. To save a center motif, such as a wonderful country scene or grouping of flowers, turn the dish over with the top facing down, then hit around the outer rim of the dish until all the pieces are broken off from the center, including the heavy circular rim the dish sits on. Turn the dish right-side up and gently try to remove any remaining rim pieces.

Using tile nippers. Tile nippers are an excellent tool to use for breaking away particular parts of the china, especially the underside rim, which is thicker than the other parts of the dish. When using tile nippers, place the cutting jaws so they overlap the edge of the tile or china, then squeeze the handles firmly and evenly. If you end up breaking the center piece, use it that way — a crack down the middle may actually enhance your design. Remember, this is all about using broken pieces, so don't let any unplanned breaks upset you.

USEFUL SIZES FOR SHARDS

The sizes you break the shards into can vary. In general, most of your shards should range from large (the size of a half dollar) to medium size (the size of a quarter), with some tiny ones (the size of a nickel). This is really a personal decision, depending on your artistic taste and the size of your base. For a larger base you can use larger pieces, and this will make the work go faster. You can mix the sizes and shapes or decide to use only large or very small pieces. Each technique has its own distinct look, so experiment.

Arranging shards is a bit like putting together the pieces of a puzzle. I like to put my pieces as close together as possible. In the French *pique assiette* tradition, the pieces are placed so close together that you can barely see a grout line. But, once again, this is a matter of personal taste (as well as quite a lot of work). You may like the look achieved when pieces are more spread out with more grout showing. Just make sure all the cracks between the shards are filled completely with grout.

You will want a good variety of shapes and types of shards to work with. It's also helpful to have a variety of curved pieces, both concave and convex, so you can match the pieces more closely to the curves of your base. Keep your eye out for unusual curved, corner, and pointed pieces that may be just right for working around a particular shape.

Before you begin working, you should sort your shards by size and color. This will enable you to have quicker access to exactly what you need as you design your piece. Use a whisk broom to clean up the small particles of shards left after breaking and save them in a separate container. These tiny shards are good for filling small spaces on any project.

LOOK BEFORE YOU BREAK

Before you break a dish, vase, or any piece, be sure to check the markings on the bottom first because it may be more valuable as an antique than as shards. There are several books on pottery markings and many dealers in fine porcelain who will be happy to assist you if you think you have a piece of some value.

STEP-BY-STEP INSTRUCTIONS

These instructions cover all of the basic steps you need to know to complete the projects in this book. Each individual project contains only tips and instructions specific to that project; refer back to these pages as you work if necessary.

PREPARATION

1. Prepare your base surface (see page 23) and set it on a lazy Susan. Apply a coat of invisible glove cream to your hands for protection.

2. Gather, break, and separate your shards. Experiment with color schemes and design ideas; sort the shards and set them aside in containers. Sweep up small shards with a whisk broom to use for fill-in work.

ATTACHING SHARDS

3. Starting with the largest sculptural piece or central element of your design, begin applying shards. Using a large craft stick, apply a small dab of mastic to the back of a shard. ▾

Then, place it in position. Press to attach firmly. Be sure not to use too much mastic; if it oozes from behind the shard when you press on it, then you have too much and it will be difficult to place shards side by side. Only when you are trying to create a flat surface and using thin shards will a thick layer of mastic be needed.

4. Apply mastic to the next shard and place it as close as possible to the first one. Remember that the mastic takes at least eight hours to dry, so if you don't like the way a design is developing, you can remove and rearrange pieces. If the mastic has dried, use a screwdriver to pop off the pieces you want to remove. ▾

Continue placing shards, working your way around or over the whole base surface until it is completely covered. If you notice small areas between shards that you want to fill in, glue tiny shard pieces into these spots.

APPLYING LARGE SCULPTURAL ELEMENTS

If you have selected some larger sculptural elements for your piece, glue these on before the small shards. You may need to support these pieces while the mastic dries, either by bracing them with small sticks or by laying the piece on its side. Allow the mastic to dry for at least eight hours before applying the remaining smaller pieces. Another option is to use a faster-drying glue, such as Bondo. The sculptural element should be fully secure before applying the grout.

5. Once all the shards are glued to the base, allow it to dry for at least eight hours.

APPLYING GROUT

6. Wearing a dust mask, place about one cup of unsanded grout in a plastic container. You may need more for larger projects. If you want colored grout, add the desired pigment to the dry grout before mixing (see page 21). Slowly add acrylic additive or water, stirring thoroughly with a craft stick. Make sure to mix in all the dry particles on the bottom of the bowl. It should have the consistency of thick mud; add more dry grout or liquid as needed. Let the grout set for about ten minutes before beginning to apply. ▼

7. Wear heavy gauge rubber gloves for protection against the grout and the china's sharp edges. Using your hands, spread the grout generously over a section of the surface. Push the grout between the shards to fill in the gaps and make a level surface between shards. ▼

Every crevice must be filled since even the slightest hole or crack will allow moisture to seep in. Rinse your hands periodically in a large bucket of water to avoid a buildup of grout on your gloves.

8. When you're finished applying grout, turn your piece on the lazy Susan to inspect it from all angles. Examine the smoothness of your grout lines between shards. These should be smooth and level with the adjoining shards. If any of the lines are pitted or rough, smooth a thin layer of grout over the grout line with your index finger. ▼

SCRAPING BACK

9. I usually remove my heavy rubber gloves at this stage to allow for greater mobility to scrape back the grout. Using a craft stick or paring knife, scrape off the heavier portions of grout from the shard surface. Be careful not to scrape out

TIPS FOR APPLYING GROUT

◆ You will have approximately one hour to work before the grout dries. Until you have a sense of how fast you can apply and clean back the grout before it hardens, start with a small batch of grout and mix more as needed.

◆ Don't be shocked by how messy the piece looks at this stage; all that grout covering your beautiful design will be cleaned off later and the luster of the shards will be restored.

◆ The best time to find and fill spots missing grout is when you have just finished grouting the entire piece, but you can go back and spot-grout even after the piece is fully dry.

any grout from between the shards. This part of the process takes a lot of time and attention to detail. Place excess grout back into the plastic container and reuse for filling spots as needed. ▼

10. When you have scraped as much grout as possible from the surface of your piece, wipe it clean with a dry terry towel. If grout is fully dry, wet the towel slightly, but do not use a very wet towel on damp grout: It will pull grout from the cracks. ▼

FINISHING

11. Allow grout on cleaned piece to dry until hard to the touch, approximately two to three hours.

12. Wearing a dust mask, use a Dremel or metal file to grind down any rough or sharp edges on your piece. ▼

Dremel

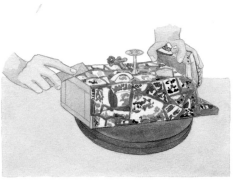
Metal file

If you discover any cracks or holes in the dried grout at this point, mix up a small batch of grout and touch up neglected areas. This is also a good time to check the smoothness of your grout lines one more time, and to use a thin layer of grout to go over any rough lines.

13. Polish the finished surface with a dry terry towel.

CLEANING UP

When using grout, the best time to clean up your equipment and work space is immediately after you are finished, when the grout is still manageable and has not completely hardened. Sweep the floor of any grout chips and wash the tabletop and floor area. Any remaining grout in the plastic container can be left to dry; it will pop out when dry and can then be easily discarded. Do not pour the water used for cleaning up the grout down your household drains; it is best to discard it outside because of the buildup of silt in the water. Rinse your hands with vinegar to restore the pH balance on your skin.

REMOVING DRIED GROUT

Grout is quite dry after just one hour. It's very important that you clean all the grout off before leaving your piece to dry. Dried grout is not impossible to remove, but cleaning is much easier when the grout is wet. If you find spots where the grout has begun to harden, use a spray bottle to mist the dried grout before scraping. This greatly increases the amount of time you have to clean your piece.

MAKING A HOME FOR
OUT-OF-COMMISSION TEAPOTS

Evelyn Ferrier of western Australia created the Tea Tree Garden in her backyard as a place to retire teapots with bad pouring spouts. She covered a wall with porcelain tea spouts, which she then converted into a fountain that actually spouts water. She also hung teapots like Christmas ornaments on a tree near the wall. And adjoining the wall is a garden that is embellished with kitchen crockery.

Ferrier says, "I hate throwing things away; just because something is broken doesn't mean it is not beautiful . . . people don't know what to do with their treasures so they bring them to me. Every piece has its own story."

Chapter Four

PROJECTS FOR THE HOME

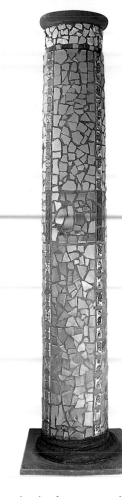

H ow you furnish and decorate your home is the ultimate expression of identity, taste, and personality — what you find beautiful, humorous, and enjoyable to be surrounded by. Bits and pieces mosaics are a wonderful way to put your own signature on your home, a kind of handwriting in junk assemblage that encompasses flair, fun, and a personal sense of style. Acknowledge the magic and explore this delightful art form as you decorate your home. Whether your home is streamlined modern or homey country, these bits and pieces surfaces will complement the decor. The choice of shards and the design scheme you develop can be tailored to set any mood and match any style.

All the projects in this chapter follow the basic step-by-step instructions described in chapter 3. Each project requires the equipment and materials discussed in chapter 2, with a few additions, as noted.

The artist is the man who creates not only for the need but for the joy, and in the long run the mankind will not be content without sharing that joy through the possession of real works of art, however humble or unpretentious they may be.

— Roger Fry

FLOWERPOT

Covering a terra-cotta flowerpot is a great beginning project. The terra-cotta is very porous and holds mastic and grout firmly. The flowerpot's simple shape and limited surface area provide a good opportunity to experiment with design and to develop your skill at fitting together the shard pieces.

Base and Materials

Terra-cotta flowerpot, any size or shape (a chipped or cracked one that might otherwise go unused is perfect)

Acrylic additive

Preparing the Base
◆ If you're recycling a pot, clean it thoroughly.

Selecting Shards
◆ Select curved shards that reflect the curve of the pot, or use small shards that can be placed closely together to follow the curves.

Assembly Tips
◆ Place smooth-edged rim pieces of china around the rim of the pot to create a finished edging.
◆ Turn the lazy Susan as you go to ensure you cover all sides of the pot.
◆ Try doing several pots in a row, using different color schemes and incorporating a variety of sculptural elements. Some that I find particularly fun to work with are large porcelain flowers, two or more cup handles arranged symmetrically around the pot or randomly across the surface, a tea spout, multicolored buttons, and pieces of junk jewelry.

Finishing Steps
◆ To give the pot a finished look, I recommend applying a smooth, thin layer of grout to the inside surface of the pot. This will also give it another layer of moisture protection. Mix a small amount of grout with acrylic additive or water to a consistency thinner than that of mud. Then, spread the grout evenly on the inside of the pot, wearing rubber gloves. ▼

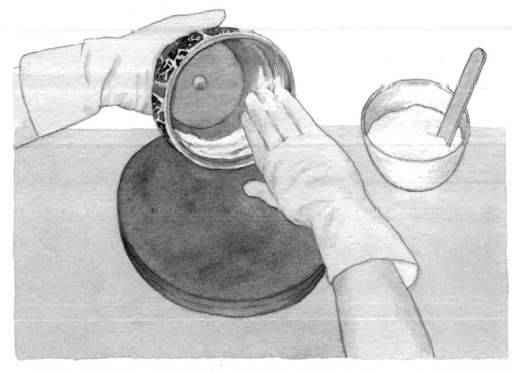

With rubber gloves on your hands, spread a thin layer of grout over the entire inside of the pot by moving the pot from side to side.

LAMP BASE

I chose this lamp base because of its shape. The flatness of the top was perfect for setting some sculptural pieces for accents. This one was in working condition, but it is easy and inexpensive to have an electrician rewire a lamp.

I made this lamp for my daughter Leigh, and the sculptural pieces were chosen with her in mind. The fat periwinkle blue handle was from a cup she had given to me for a Mother's Day present. I also included a porcelain girl's head, glass marbles, and china pieces with a mixture of great blues, and added an accent piece of a dark purple cluster of grapes.

Base

Lamp base (with properly working electrical elements)

◆ Remember that when the finished lamp is turned on, the shards are spotlighted. In making this lamp, I decided to use the most interesting pieces of glass I could collect, particularly cut glass and pieces with wonderful colors.

Preparing the Base

◆ Lamp bases are usually made of ceramic and are not very porous. The surface will need to be sanded lightly to enable the glue to adhere more easily. Applying a very thin layer of mastic will give the surface additional grip. Wearing rubber gloves, smooth the mastic over the base with your finger.

Assembly Tip

◆ As you apply shards, leave the area where the the wire comes out of the base open enough for the wire to move freely.

Selecting Shards

◆ Choosing shards that have a curve similar to that of the base will make covering the surface easier. Small shards cover curves much more easily than large ones; have some very small shards on hand to ease around the shape. ▶

Mailbox

Neighbors, visitors, and passersby will notice a mailbox covered with shards. I used a metal wall-mounted mailbox for this particular project, although any style will work.

I try to create a consistent mood with both the colors and forms I choose for a piece. In this case, I created a country feel by starting with a flat ceramic cow, which dictated the theme. I added a spout to one end and a handle at the other give the mailbox a teapot look. I also used a wooden kitchen spoon and porcelain flowers and vegetables, along with bright primary colors, especially barn red, to complete the whimsical country style.

Base

Metal or wooden mailbox (either house-mounted or post-mounted style)

Preparing the Base

◆ Make sure the mailbox surface is clean. If it is painted, give the surface a light sanding with coarse sandpaper. Wearing rubber gloves, apply a very thin layer of mastic with your finger over the entire surface to create a texture that will hold the bond. Let dry for at least a few hours.

Selecting Shards

◆ Be sure that your sculptural elements and shards will not interfere with the opening and closing of the mailbox. ▶

Finishing Step

◆ If the mailbox will be exposed to weather, a clear water sealant should be applied for additional protection against the elements.

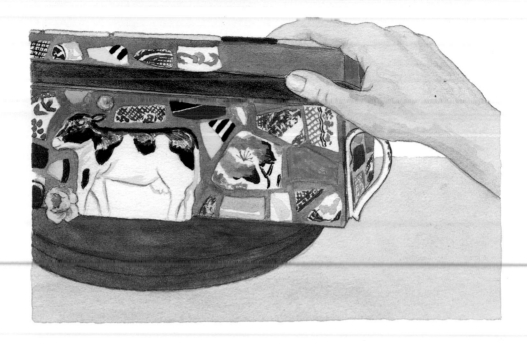

ASSEMBLY OPTION

A post-mounted mailbox has its own unique challenges and opportunities for creativity:

◆ If the mailbox has a flag, be sure that no shards interfere with its function. You'll probably find that you'll have to leave the area surrounding the flag uncovered.

◆ The post itself can be a surface for applying shards. Make sure to finish with a coat of water sealant; it will protect the post from water damage.

The magical thinker creates new myths from odds and ends of old ones, from shards of individuals and collective history.

— Claude Lévi-Strauss

UMBRELLA STAND

This is a clever use of the terra-cotta cylinders that are found in any building materials store. On this piece I used a lot of sculptural elements: a large white cherub, a tureen handle, a figurine of a dog, tea spouts, large decorative cup handles, and porcelain flowers. I used multiple colors, trying to mix as many complementary colors as possible.

Base and Materials

Terra-cotta container 8" x 8" square and 26" high

One 12" x 12" piece of ½" to 1" plywood

6" tile square

Bondo

Water sealant

Preparing the Base

◆ To construct the base, center and glue the six-inch tile onto the piece of plywood, using mastic. ▾

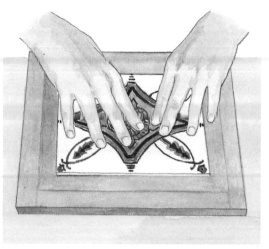

Attach the terra-cotta container to the plywood base by applying Bondo around the bottom edge of the container and pressing onto the plywood square. Bondo will dry within seconds; the shards can then be glued on. ▶

Assembly Tips

◆ The terra-cotta is very porous and will hold the bond well. Cover both the terra-cotta and the plywood base with shards.

◆ As in the garden wall project on page 69, I used Bondo to apply the large elements. Bondo is highly toxic, so use only in a well-ventilated area and follow the directions carefully. Bondo dries very quickly, so mix only the amount you need for one item at a time.

Finishing Step

◆ Paint on a clear water sealant to protect the surfaces inside and out.

FRUIT BOWL

A shard-covered bowl makes a charming centerpiece for any table. Any type of bowl can be covered, but a wooden bowl is best because it is porous. In this project, I used an older wooden bowl, covering only the inside surface.

I chose dishes in a warm pink floral pattern that seemed to blend well with a soft blue. I used a small porcelain rose to continue the soft pink color scheme, a crystal stopper, and a small white porcelain figurine head for some whimsy.

Base

Bowl, wooden or other material such as metal or ceramic

Preparing the Base

◆ Make sure the surface is free of grease and dirt. If the surface has been painted, a light sanding will help improve the bond.

Selecting Shards

◆ The inside of a bowl is concave. Find china with similar shapes, such as bowls or cups with a patterned inside. If the china's curve fits comfortably with the shape of the bowl, the finished surface will be more cohesive. Using very small shards will also make the curve easier to cover fully. ▶

◆ Even on a concave surface, sculptural elements can still be enjoyed: A small head, miniature rose, or a marble will not interfere with the general use of the bowl.

MIRROR

Mirrors bring light into a home, expand the perceived space, and offer reflections of the people who live there.

I bought this mirror very cheaply at a thrift shop because of the poor condition of the glass. If you find a used mirror that reflects relatively well, you may want to preserve the vintage look. However, if you do need to replace it, a glass shop can cut a mirror to fit.

For this piece, I was inspired by the grouping of porcelain flowers, which I applied first. I also used a large piece of broken Tiffany glass from the edge of a vase, a glass flower, a cluster of glass grapes, and a delicate porcelain pitcher.

Preparing the Base

◆ Make sure your mirror frame is free of any dirt or loose paint. Lightly sand the surface with a coarse sandpaper. If possible, remove the mirror from the frame to prevent scratching.

◆ Use a flat board on top of the lazy Susan as a work surface to support a large mirror. This will enable you to reach all areas of the frame, working the entire surface at once.

Selecting Shards

◆ Select any sculptural elements you plan to use before you begin the assembly. You might want to look for porcelain flowers, glass perfume bottles, vintage metal compacts (used for powder), small flower vases, or pottery figurines.

Assembly Tips

◆ Apply mastic to the sculptural elements or focal points you have selected and glue these pieces into position first. ▼

◆ As you cover the inner side of frame that rests against the mirror, be sure that the pieces do not extend past the edge so that the mirror will fit properly into the frame. ▼

◆ As you scrape back the excess grout on the shards, use a paring knife first, but then try using a thin wooden skewer for reaching into tight spaces or spots where shards lie underneath protruding pieces.

Base and Materials

Wooden mirror frame

Picture wire

Brown paper

Eye hooks

Paper glue

Thin wooden skewer

Finishing Steps

◆ Turn the mirror over onto a fat pillow to keep the sculptural elements from breaking while you add the finishing touches.

◆ Replace the mirror in the frame and secure. Cut a piece of brown craft paper to cover the back and glue to the frame to protect the back of the mirror from scratches. Screw in eye hooks (choose the appropriate size for the weight of the mirror) and attach picture wire. Your mirror is ready to hang. ▼

FIREPLACE

A fireplace is usually the focal point of a room, and a new surface of broken shards and bits of shiny things gives an added warmth to the area.

I used a lot of vintage green tile for the main color in this project, then added smaller dark green tiles to create several diamond patterns across the main panel. The small orange tiles create color contrast. On the side columns I used some gold-colored bits of discarded wooden frames and dotted the center diamonds with large green glass marbles. The blue mirror pieces and dark wine tile add interest.

Base

Brick fireplace and/or wooden mantel

Fireproof Durlock concrete board (optional)

Preparing the Base

Fireplaces may have wood or brick surfaces, and some may have both. Any of these surfaces can be covered: Consider decorating just one panel across the center, the entire wood surface, or all of the wood and the brick. I have also designed and covered two floor-to-ceiling brick walls behind freestanding fireplaces. It is your decision as to how much will be covered. In this project I have covered just the woodwork around the fireplace, leaving the brick exposed.

◆ To prepare the woodwork around the fireplace, first sand the surface with a coarse sandpaper, making sure to remove any loose paint. Then score with a knife or sharp object, cutting lines down across the entire surface. This will enhance the bond of the glue. ▼

Assembly Tips

◆ Lay out your design on a flat surface close to your project. Remember that your design can be changed even after gluing until the mastic is completely dry. ▾

ASSEMBLY OPTION

◆ As an alternative technique, consider applying shards to a presized fireproof concrete board, then mounting the board onto the fireplace.

◆ Prepare the concrete board by sanding it with sandpaper then scoring it with a knife. Use a strong glue, such as Bondo, to attach the decorated board to the fireplace. ▾

◆ As you apply the shards with mastic, concentrate on your sculptural elements first. Because of their weight, they will need more attention. Sculptural pieces can be supported better by surrounding them with flatter shards, which help to support the heavier sculptural elements. You may need a faster-drying glue, such as epoxy or an industrial-strength clear adhesive. ▸

THE WEDDING BOWL POT

The pieces of this flowerpot were originally part of a treasured brown and green glazed bowl that Jim and Chris Scrimgeour received as a wedding present. Jim even wrote a poem about the bowl on their twenty-fifth wedding anniversary.

When their son and his fiancée came for a visit to announce their engagement, Jim brought out the bowl to show to the bride. He set it down briefly on a shelf with a shaky leg support. Then — you guessed it! — the entire shelf came down and the beautiful bowl shattered. They picked up the pieces and saved them, since they could not bring themselves to throw the vestiges of this favorite gift away.

When Jim and Chris told their daughter of the catastrophe, she brought the pieces to me. Now, the spirit of the wedding bowl is reincarnated in this flowerpot, which once again holds a place of honor in their home.

'Still Life in a Small Kitchen'
The wedding bowl, glazed, fired in Greece,
sits in the center of the oval table, sits on the brand new
checkered tablecloth, on
reddish-brown checks with traces of silver —
the rich soil brown bowl filled with fruit —
apples, pears, prune-plums, a bunch of bananas, and
one large peach with silver fuzz and streaks of sunrise
and sunset —
and forest green spirals on the inside of the bowl visible
in the odd spaces between fruit, swirls and whirls,
twenty-five years old —
the bowl, still intact,
still holding sweet fruit, still life in the center of our
small kitchen.

— Jim Scrimgeour

KITCHEN BACKSPLASH

What would be more appropriate for a kitchen than a backsplash of homey shards? For my friend Janet, an artist who works with recycled bottlecaps, I created this backsplash with her red kitchen sink and Blue Willow china collection in mind. Janet supplied some vintage elements: tin spice cans, old jelly glasses that her daughter had given her, plastic dollhouse furniture, and a plate that said NEW JERSEY, where she was raised.

Base and Materials

Clean plasterboard wall

Scoring knife

Acrylic additive

Water sealant

Preparing the Base

◆ To prepare the wall for gluing, score the plasterboard by running the scoring knife in long lines down the wall. This will enable the bond to hold securely. ▼

Selecting Shards

◆ Develop an idea for a color pattern and select your pieces before beginning. Prepare many similar-size shard pieces of each color.

◆ Select the sculptural elements you think would work nicely as focus points of your design and lay them out on the counter near the wall area where you envision placing them. Elements such as whole plates broken into sections, eating utensils, and other kitchenware are especially appropriate for this project. Choose more elements than you think you will need because as you begin to hold them up to the selected places on the wall (before gluing), you may well discover that one piece does not fit as well as you thought it would. Before you glue is the time to decide on the best sculptural elements to enhance your creation.

Assembly Tips

◆ Glue on the large sculptural elements first and let them dry. Some of the pieces may need some additional support so they don't slide while the glue is drying. You may want to use heavier glue on these pieces. ▶

◆ Glue the shards around the sculptural elements, building on your design. I recommend working on several areas of the wall simultaneously so that the overall design is cohesive and balanced. This process may take several days if the surface area you are covering is very large.

◆ Mix the grout with acrylic additive in place of water to protect it from moisture.

◆ When applying grout around the sculptural elements, be sure to fill in the large gaps and build a supportive base with the grout to further strengthen the bond and to support the added weight of the sculptural piece.

◆ Remember when applying grout to such a large area that it is best to work on small sections at a time so the grout is manageable. You can buy more time by misting the grouted area with water. If you are working with colored grout, mix a large amount of dry grout with colored pigment in order to have consistent color throughout the project.

Finishing Step

◆ Although the acrylic additive in the grout provides a moisture barrier, you can coat the entire surface with a clear water sealant to provide additional protection from any water breaking down the bond.

THE BLOOMSBURY CHINA

When they hear the word *Bloomsbury*, most people think of the novels of Virginia Woolf and E. M. Forster. The literary side of this prominent artistic circle certainly continues to dominate the Bloomsbury image, but the truth is that two highly unusual studio artists and two controversial art critics were among Bloomsbury's inner nucleus. Vanessa Bell, Duncan Grant, Roger Fry, and Clive Bell were significant in breaking down the artistic conventions of the early twentieth century in England. One of the media they worked in was china shards.

In 1911, Vanessa Bell wrote Roger Fry asking for any mosaic pieces left over from a mosaic wall project that he and Duncan Grant had worked on at Roger's house in Durbins. "We are busy . . . making a small cemented place to sit out on and we're going to make a small inlaid piece of mosaic of odd bits of china, glass, etc. in the center and also a narrow border round the edge. . . . The border will be only about three or four inches wide and five feet square so not much would be wanted only I think one ought to have some one or two colors running through the medley of bits of china, etc.," wrote Bell. This seat would become one of their earliest experimentations in bits and pieces mosaics.

In 1932, they continued their work with china when the Wedgwood company commissioned Duncan Grant and Vanessa Bell to decorate sets of dinner service. They produced a vast array of plates painted with portrait heads of famous women — from Marie Antoinette to Charlotte Brontë, from Elizabeth I to "Miss 1933" — and of the two artists. These designs were painted on white-glazed Wedgwood plates and then fired.

Chapter Five

Projects for the Garden

Gardens are meant to provide a domestic haven and intimate shelter. They offer a refuge from the stress of modern life, a place to let the mind rest and the imagination soar. Bits and pieces mosaic is the perfect medium for the imagination to work and play in, and for adding joyous creations to the garden. Gardening and shards of china both represent two important elements of domestic life: the necessities and the passion. What could be more enjoyable in a garden than a memory lane for all to delight in?

Bits and pieces can be created on a modest or a grand scale, depending on the style and size of your outdoor space. These delightful shard art pieces create intriguing new effects for any garden. You can create pieces for a wildflower garden or a formal garden, for a large patio or a small balcony. So let your imagination run wild and enjoy the process of creating art for your garden.

Imagination is more important

than knowledge.

— Albert Einstein

BIRDBATH

A birdbath offers a serene spot to watch the birds enjoy their baths or have an occasional drink. The pleasure can be doubled when your birdbath's surface is covered with homey dish shards and glittering elements.

For this project, designed by Linda Benswanger, a plate with a bluebird on it was broken and then reglued at the center of the birdbath. You may choose to place a sculptural element, such as a big porcelain flower or bird, at the center of the bowl.

Base and Materials

Cement birdbath

Water sealant

Acrylic additive

where the water will freeze in the bowl, move the birdbath indoors or turn it upside down in the winter, because the shards and glues will not survive these conditions.

Preparing the Base

◆ You can purchase simple bird-bath forms at most garden centers or, if you feel daring, marry any shallow bowl to a stand and create your own base form. A concrete birdbath form does not need much preparation, but if you are creating your own, select a stand that is sturdy enough to support the bowl.

Selecting Shards

Select an interesting sculptural element for the center of the birdbath along with the rest of your shards. The inside of the birdbath bowl is concave, so it is best to look for china that will have a similar curve, such as the insides of bowls or cups. The stand will require shards with an opposite curve, so use pieces like the outsides of bowls or cups. These curved pieces of china will follow the contours of your base nicely. Small shards placed close together are another way to follow the curves.

Assembly Tips

◆ Mix grout with acrylic additive.

◆ Be careful not to apply shards too close to the area of the base where the bowl will rest.

◆ Thoroughly fill in all cracks and crevices with grout because the bowl will be filled with water. There should not be even a pinhole for water to get into, or the bond will eventually be loosened. If you live in a colder climate

Finishing Steps

◆ Paint on a clear coat of water sealant for double protection.

◆ Put the stand in a level spot in your garden and place the bowl on the stand. ▾

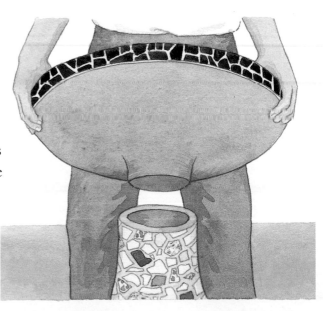

BIRDHOUSE

A bits and pieces birdhouse makes a delightful accent piece for your yard or garden. You can find inexpensive, unfinished wooden birdhouses at garden centers or almost any home supply store. The raw wood is porous, making it a a perfect surface on which to apply mastic and grout.

I had been saving the roof portion of a broken house-shaped teapot and half of the top of an antique sugar bowl until just the right project came along. These two items inspired the roof of the birdhouse, which in turn inspired the rest of the project. I used a wonderful antique brass curtain tieback for the birds' perch.

Base

Any style of wooden birdhouse

Preparing the Base

◆ The porous wood of an unfinished birdhouse does not need much preparation for applying bits and pieces, but if you are refinishing a painted birdhouse, lightly sand the surface.

Selecting Shards

◆ Shards with right angles can be especially useful in covering corners.

Assembly Tips

◆ When applying grout, be sure to smooth grout lines along the corner edges to create crisp corners between the abutting shards. ▶

◆ Turn the birdhouse upside down: A different vantage point can reveal cracks that aren't filled.

WATERING CAN

This very charming container I designed for my daughter Marlo, a horticulturist, to use for all her watering tasks. I found this old watering can at a yard sale for only a few dollars. I was especially happy that some of the old red paint remained on the spout. I let the red paint lead the color scheme and found some wonderful yellow plates to accent it. I used a cluster of small flowers as the sculptural element.

Base

Metal watering can

Preparing the Base

◆ Clean the watering can's surface. If the can has been painted, remove any flaking paint or paint chips with coarse sandpaper.

Selecting Shards

◆ Porcelain flowers set in the center create a garden theme. Flowered dishes can be used to continue the theme.

Assembly Tip

◆ If you plan to use the watering can, make sure that the shards and the grouting on the handle are smooth enough to be held comfortably.

GOOD LUCK SHARDS

There is an old European custom, called in German *Polterabend,* that traditionally takes place the evening before a wedding ceremony. The wedding guests come to visit and party with the bride and groom. As part of the custom, each guest brings along a piece of china. When the bride and groom greet each guest at the door, the guest breaks the china on the front doorstep for good luck. The groom is then expected to sweep up the broken china to prove he will be able to take care of his bride when they are married. The more china brought and broken on the doorstep, the more luck bestowed upon the marriage.

The mother of one German bride brought me all the broken china from a prewedding dinner. Out of these good luck shards I created a large garden urn that the mother gave to her daughter as a gift. Now she will have all these good luck shards (a piece from every guest) to enjoy and to pass down to her family, passing on the custom, the story, and plenty of good luck.

*Anyone can do anything with a
million dollars — look at Disney.
But it takes more than money
to make something out of
nothing, and look at the fun
I have doing it.*

— Grandma Prisbrey, folk artist

PLANT STAND

You can build your own stand out of wood or buy any type of plant stand in almost any material for this project. I found this one at a tag sale. It had some interesting wood carving near the top, which I decided to leave exposed. I used many decorative cup handles all down the pole, and on the top I glued a lovely pastoral scene I salvaged from a vintage plate.

Base

Wooden or metal plant stand

Preparing the Base
◆ Make sure there is no loose paint on the plant stand.

Selecting Shards
◆ The top of this plant stand is flat and the shards need to lay as flat and even as possible, so choose shards with similar thicknesses.
◆ The column is convex and will need to have shards with a complementary curve. If your supply of curved china is limited, break the shards into very small shapes that will follow the curve more easily.

Assembly Tip
◆ To create a flat surface for the top of the plant stand, use different amounts of mastic to compensate for the varying thicknesses of the dish shards. ▼

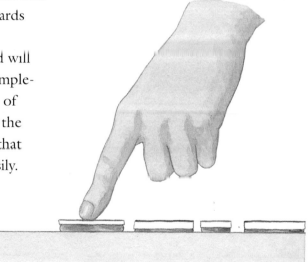

BRINGING COLOR TO THE LANDSCAPE

Robert Bellamy, a Dallas landscape designer, was inspired to incorporate bits and pieces into the design of his own home and garden after seeing Gaudí's mirror-and-glass-encrusted Sagrada Familia church in Barcelona. "A Crayola wonderland of color and undulating shapes" is how Bellamy described Gaudí's work.

Creating debris-laden surfaces that incorporated Fiesta flatware and rummaged tile and deco glass, Bellamy transformed his house and yard. The entrance wall to his garden is a sinuous line of shards with a wildly wonderful band of color that stretches the full length of the top of the wall. It is embedded with deco glass, creating a "dinosaur back" just before the entrance gate. Bellamy says, "What could be more compelling in a garden?"

THE GARDEN WALKWAY

This is a very simple but rewarding surface to create with shards. The finished walkway should be flat and level because it will get some amount of use and must be walkable. This is a charming addition to a garden, and the stone and dish shards complement each other perfectly.

These stones were designed and created by Linda Benswanger. Her work has been inspired by both the Victorian-style mosaics from the 1920s and the Byzantine mosaics. Her business Mozayiks, established in 1991, mainly sells birdhouses, birdbaths, and garden-related items to retail stores, but often will do custom installations, backsplashes, tables, and floors. She recently moved her business from Manhattan to Germantown, New York, where she enjoys her new country surroundings.

Base

Garden stepping-stones (any size of flat stones will work)

Preparing the Base

◆ The stones for this project can be purchased at garden centers, but you could use any flat stone for your walkway. You could work with different sizes, if you wish, and create your own pattern.

Selecting Shards

◆ Try to use shards of similar thickness, in order to create a flat surface. If there are special shards that are very thin compared to other shards being used on this project, raise their height with added mastic. ▶

Assembly Tip

◆ Continually check the flatness of the surface as you glue on the shards.

ASSEMBLY OPTIONS

◆ Find any flat garden stones or groups of flat stones and treat the surface exactly the same.
◆ Shards can be embedded into a walkway just after the cement has been poured and is still wet. Keep in mind that the walkway must be level for people to walk on it.
◆ I have even used shards as mulch in flower beds.

THE GARDEN TABLE

A table made with broken tiles and dishes provides a whimsical way to enjoy summer meals on a porch or in a sunroom. The original idea for this table came from an interior designer who commissioned me to create a garden table that incorporated six expensive new Italian dinner plates. On this table I modified the design and used six different vintage plates, first breaking them then reassembling them on the table surface. In the center I set a floral design to give the feel of looking down at a set table with a flower arrangement.

I made the first table on a forty-eight-inch round base of pressed plywood, which turned out to be a big design flaw. Outside on the patio the plywood absorbed large amounts of water, eventually swelling and cracking the surface. Remember this when making your own table — either use a nonporous base or plan to use your table only indoors.

Base and Materials

48" round top with a decorative sturdy base

Six similar-size dinner plates

Multicolored tiles

Bondo

Dremel

Water sealant

Preparing the Base

◆ Measure out and mark the spacing for the dinner plates, arranging them approximately where they would be if dinner was being served. On this table, the plates are eight inches apart and two and one-half inches from the edge. These measurements will dictate how much room you will have left over for the center design (in this case, about twenty-four inches). Use a marker to delineate the place for each of these focal points. ▶

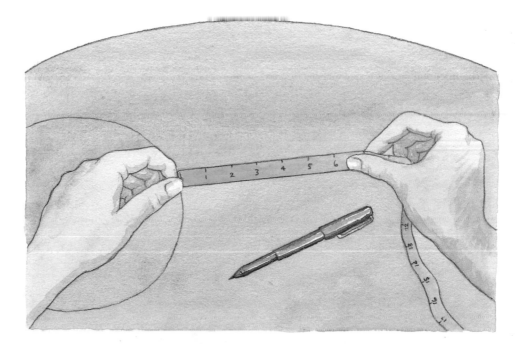

Selecting Shards

◆ Choose six matching or complementary plates of approximately the same size.

◆ Remove as much as you can of the heavy bottom rim of the plates with tile nippers, working on only one plate at a time. To keep your pieces intact for easy reconstruction, attach self-adhesive paper to the back of each whole plate.

◆ Turn each plate facedown on a wooden block and hammer the edges first. Try to break the plate so that the edges will lie as flat as possible. ▼

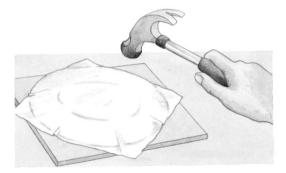

◆ Note the thickness of the dinner plates and select other bits and pieces that are about the same thickness. The finished surface must be smooth and even, and if your plates are much thicker than your tiles it will be difficult to make them even with mastic.

◆ Break all the tiles for the rest of the surface design separately and place in a container to have at your disposal.

Assembly Tips

◆ Place your tabletop on a large piece of fabric to enable you to turn it as you work.

◆ Place the broken plates in the positions marked out for them. Then, apply some broken tile pieces around the plates. The height of these pieces can be adjusted by using more or less mastic to make them level with the dinner plates. ▼

◆ As an added strengthener, use Bondo to apply the tiles along the edge of the table. It will help these tiles withstand daily use.

◆ When applying the grout make sure to fill in every crack, especially along the edge and under the broken-tile outer rim of the table. This area will receive the most abuse and should be thoroughly sealed.

◆ Since the surface is flat, you can scrape back the grout with any long, flat tool such as a piece of sturdy cardboard, plastic (sold in tile stores), or even a dry terry towel.

Finishing Steps

◆ The broken tiles and dinner plates may have some sharp edges. Feel across the tabletop with your bare hands and use a Dremel or metal file to smooth any sharp edges.

◆ Paint an invisible coat of water sealant both on the top and under the bottom of the table to give it added protection to withstand daily use.

BITS & PIECES FROM THE SEA

When you pick up a pretty seashell on the beach, you may not realize that you are following a tradition that stretches back at least as far as the Renaissance. The history of shells as exquisite objects to be gathered and traded, hoarded and displayed, can be traced to the collectors of the sixteenth and seventeenth centuries; cabinets of these curiosities existed in almost every European palace across the Continent. To those first enthusiasts, the appeal of magical pearly surfaces and complex natural geometrics proved as irresistible as it is today to the artist, the scientist, or the child filling a bucket at the seaside.

The earliest serious collectors sought the choicest individual specimens. At the same time, shells were beginning to be used for decorative or architectural effects. A number of avant-garde patrons, at first in Italy, but soon all over Europe, created whole rooms ornamented with both common and exotic varieties arranged in intricate patterns on walls and other surfaces. Although such shell work was originally considered most appropriate for the interiors of grottoes, bathhouses, and garden buildings, enough shell rooms survive inside grand houses to demonstrate how influential the idea was.

SMALL GARDEN WALL

The base of this garden wall is a recycled sculpture made by an artist whose studio was in the same building as mine. One day while visiting the Dumpster, I found it abandoned and decided the form would make a wonderful small accent wall.

The sculpture has a wooden armature covered with chicken wire, then wrapped in cheesecloth. The final layer is a coating of Structo-Lite, a perlited gypsum plaster, which can be purchased at any home building supply store. Although the sculpture was designed to stand vertically, I decided to put it in a horizontal position to create this small wall for a garden.

Although the inspiration was instant, the structure lay outside my studio for several years waiting for its new life. I had to repair the cement surface a bit before I could begin work on my long-awaited creation. Because of its size, I set it on a large wooden box with a large lazy Susan (made to hold a television in a home entertainment center) on top. This allowed me to view all sides as I worked.

Base and Materials

Base form

Pliers

Structo-Lite or any type of thin-set mortar

Decorative iron

Bondo

Water sealant

Preparing the Base

◆ If the base form has been exposed to winter weather or needs repairing, apply a skim coat of Structo-Lite.

Selecting Shards

◆ This project requires a tremendous number of shards. On such a large job, keeping the shards color-coded will facilitate the design flow.

◆ Gather all the sculptural elements you wish to include. For this wall, I chose to put some old decorative iron on top to add some height. When dealing with heavier sculptural elements, the stability of these pieces must be worked out properly. The sculptural elements should not collect water, which could loosen the mastic bond.

Assembly Tips

◆ Because the base structure I used was covered with chicken wire, I attached the decorative iron with wire. But you could mount the iron and other sculptural elements with Bondo, a filler for car surfaces. Use Bondo in a well-ventilated area, mixing only enough for one item at a time, as it hardens very quickly. ▼

◆ Apply the sculptural elements first, beginning with the largest ones. Allow the mastic or Bondo to dry thoroughly, then apply the shards.

◆ When working on such a large surface, scoop up a handful of grout (which should be the texture of thick mud) and push it into the crevices between the shards and the sculptural elements. Make sure to fill in heavily around the sculptural elements to give the weight of the sculptural piece added support. It is best to work a small area at a time.

VARIATIONS ON A GARDEN WALL

It is not possible for everyone to find a discarded sculpture to cover. But with a little imagination you can use all kinds of recycled materials to create authentic and inventive elements, be it a garden sculpture or anything else you can dream up. Usually the magic is worked around the found object, which is transmuted from junk to art. The idea that you can be creative with disposable junk is exciting, and it makes sense to recycle what is broken or no longer wanted. Here are a couple of ideas.

Build a Base ▶

Design a wall that is just the right size to fit in your garden, then have a carpenter build a wooden base structure to fit your design. Cement cinder blocks can also be grouped to use as a base for creating an accent wall.

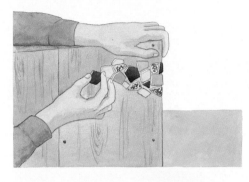

Cover an Existing Wall or Chimney ▶

I have always wanted to cover an existing chimney — I have two very ugly cinder block chimneys side by side on my house, and a new shard surface would be a definite face-lift. Don't think you have to cover the entire chimney: I have a friend who just attached a dish that belonged to her grandmother to the center of her chimney and left the rest of the chimney as is.

For this project, like the other outdoor projects, I would use a cement made with an acrylic additive, which would help the mosaics with-

stand severe weather in cold climates. Most chimneys are made of brick or stucco, so the shards can be glued directly onto the surface. I have found that a brick surface is the easiest to cover because the bricks are so porous — they hold the mastic almost immediately.

GRANDMA PRISBREY'S BOTTLE VILLAGE

When Tressa "Grandma" Prisbrey, a self-taught artist, began her Bottle Village in 1956 at the age of sixty, her sole purpose was to build a place to store her collection of dolls and seventeen thousand pencils. Today, Grandma Prisbrey's Bottle Village covers a third of an acre, complete with wishing wells, garden walls, and her "houses" — all made from objects found at the dump and glued together with mortar. Grandma Prisbrey transformed junk into a new kind of life.

The Bottle Village is the ultimate creative recycling, using car headlights, medical tubes, fire screens, and, of course, bottles. In her collection are fifteen bottle houses, which are made from more than 100 thousand whole bottles placed in mortar. The rumor has it that Grandma Prisbrey had a husband who consumed a lot of alcohol, which is how she acquired the huge number of bottles used in her creations.

The Bottle Village, located in Simi Valley, California, is now considered a significant folk-art environment because of its use of recycled mass consumer throwaways from everyday lives, an unusual medium for the 1950s and early 1960s. Because of Prisbrey's original creative output and labor, her Bottle Village has earned the status of Cultural Landmark in the state of California. Grandma Prisbrey's Bottle Village is also listed on the National Register of Historic Places and is now cared for by a private nonprofit entity. It is open to the public.

Chapter Six

BITS & PIECES OF THE IMAGINATION

Now that you've mastered the basic technique, I hope you will use this medium to explore your own inventiveness and push even wider the already loose boundaries of this improvisational art form. Bits and pieces can be brought into every aspect of your life — from what you wear to where you sit, from small pieces to enjoy in the privacy of your home to large public pieces for the enjoyment of everyone who passes by them daily, from cherished personalized gifts for others to the most personal expression of yourself for all time. Once you begin looking at the objects in your home, your garden, and even your car and office as potential surfaces for applying bits and pieces, these places will not be the same again.

I've also included the work of several other bits and pieces mosaic artists in this chapter to show how various design tastes, imaginations, and materials produce quite different finished pieces. Your own pieces are sure to bear the distinct mark of your personal style and aesthetics as well.

Trust that still, small voice that says 'This might work and I'll try it.'

— Diane Mariechild

JEWELRY

Making jewelry from your favorite shards is a quick fix for the creative urge. Rather than putting pieces together, all you have to do is select one of your favorite shards and most of the work is done. These pieces make wonderful gifts, as well as great permanent parts of your own jewelry collection. When I wear my pottery pins, people always remark on the uniqueness of having a piece of your favorite dish or the family china pattern as part of your wardrobe.

Base and Materials

Pin, earring, and barrette backs

Wire mesh file or brick

Clear industrial-strength glue

Roll of copper foil, available at craft supply stores

Soldering iron, available at craft supply stores

Solder (the best combination is 60% tin and 40% lead)

Selecting Shards

◆ Look for something unusual in the shards you pick for jewelry, such as an interesting pattern, a beautiful motif or scene, or an attractive shape. When you break your shards keep in mind the size needed, as well as the design you are trying to create.

◆ Lighter-weight shards are best for jewelry. An overly heavy pin will pull the fabric of your clothing forward, while heavy earrings or barrettes will not be comfortable to wear for long periods of time.

◆ **Pin:** Medium-size shards, about the size of a half dollar, are best for making pins. You can also join several smaller shards together edge to edge to create a multiple shard, but be careful that the pin does not become too heavy.

◆ **Earrings:** For earrings, try to find two shards that are similar in size and about the size of a quarter, so there is room for attaching the backing.

◆ **Barrettes:** A barrette back is curved, so you need shards that mimic this curve. It takes about three medium size shards to cover the full barrette back; select three that follow the curve and complement each other in shape and color.

Assembly Tips

◆ Grind the edges of the shards using a wire mesh file, often used on tiles, or a brick. The edges of shards used for jewelry need to be exceptionally smooth, so spend some extra time on this step. ▼

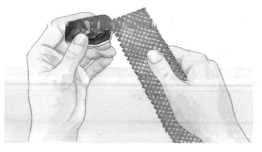

◆ Put a small dab of glue on the pin back, earring back, or barrette. Place on the shard, press, and hold until the glue hardens, about five minutes. Remove any excess glue from the shard before it hardens.

Pin: Center the back left to right, but keep it close to the top of

STAIRWAY OF MEMORIES

Kara Varian Baker, a jewelry designer whose hand-carved creations are sold at Bergdorf Goodman and Barneys in New York City, renovated an old factory building in northern California as her workshop. She filled the trim around a freestanding stucco stairway with shards from her pottery collection, which was broken in the 1986 California earthquake. "A lot of the pottery has meaning for me," she says. "I'll walk up the stairs and think, 'Ah, yes, I loved that plate.'"

the shard, otherwise the pin will not lie flat.

Earrings: Center the backing from side to side, close to the top edge of the shard.

Barrettes: Barrettes involve a little more engineering than pins because of the slight curve of the barrette backing. Place your selected pieces so that the shards fit tightly together while also following the curve of the backing. They must be glued both to the backing and to each other. ▼

Finishing Steps

◆ Applying copper foil to the edges of the shards gives the jewelry a finished look. Uncurl the foil and attach it securely to the edge your shard, peeling back the protective paper backing as you go. ▼

Handle the foil as little as possible; too much handling will cause it to lose its adhesive quality. When you have edged the entire shard, cut the foil so that the edges meet.

◆ Lay the jewelry flat or place it in a vise. Plug in the soldering iron. When it is hot, touch the tip of the iron to the copper foil, lightly melting the solder onto the foil. Rub the soldering iron across the surface to make a smooth finish. ▼

Caution: The soldering iron is hot enough to burn skin, so handle it with care.

◆ If you prefer not to use solder, you can paint the shard edges with gold or silver paint or any enamel paint to give them a finished look.

CHILDREN'S PROJECT: MAKING PINS

Shard jewelry is a great project for children ages eight and up. They are amazed that, for once, it is okay to break a dish! Make sure that they know that the edges are sharp and they must handle the shards carefully. A definite must is that they wear safety goggles when they break the dish. A brick is the safest and simplest tool for children to use to grind down the edges of the shards.

This project is great for kids because there is immediate gratification — they all go home with jewelry they created with their own hands. In my experiences making jewelry with children, I was surprised by their creativity. They came up with designs that I had not even thought about!

Base and Materials

Pin backs

Clear fast-drying glue

Brick

Acrylic paint

Paintbrush

Selecting Shards

◆ Wrap a piece of canvas or strong fabric around the pottery and place on a wooden block or sturdy surface. Have the children wear safety goggles when breaking the dishes with a hammer.

◆ The edges of the shards need to be very smooth to be worn as jewelry. Grind down the edges with a brick.

◆ Let the child free with the design. Offer some guidance about what is structurally possible and let the child take it from there. ▼

Assembly Tips

◆ The pin back needs to be centered side to side with the clasp on the left, and placed close to the top of the shard so that the pin lies flat. Make sure the pin back is snapped closed so that the child does not prick his or her fingers. Mark the placement of the pin back on each child's shard before bringing out the glue. ▼

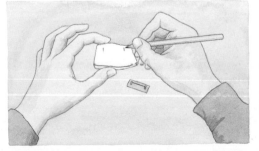

◆ Place the glue directly on the pin back. A small dab of glue is sufficient for bonding. Place the pin back on the shard and hold in place for about five minutes.

Finishing Step

◆ After the glue is completely dry, the edges of the china can be painted with acrylic paint. ▼

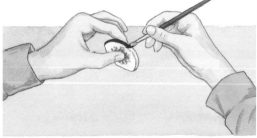

CHAIR BACKS

The key to success for this project is to find the right kind of chairs. The back of the chair should have a wooden frame that is about an inch thick. The other main factor is finding an upholsterer who is willing to work with you. Usually this type of chair back would be upholstered on both sides, but for this project, only the front gets padding and fabric. This leaves the back to serve as a base for the mosaic.

Base and Materials

**Upholstered chair with a heavy
  wooden frame**

Tempered masonite

Heavy-gauge plastic

Fabric

Pliers

Staple gun

Preparing the Base

◆ Strip the chair back of any padding or webbing. Cover the back of the wooden frame with fabric, using staples. This fabric will serve as an accent between the mosaic and the upholstery. Cover the fabric with a piece of heavy-gauge plastic and staple the edges in place to protect from glue or grout.

◆ Staple a scored piece of tempered masonite to the front of the chair back; the scoring will allow for a slight bend to follow the curve of the chair back. ▼

Selecting Shards

◆ Gather your dishes and any sculptural elements to be considered for your chair back design. You will need enough of the same colors and sculptural elements to make a fair match if you want to make a set.

Assembly Tips

◆ First apply any sculptural elements with mastic. You may need to support the weight with a stick until the mastic dries. The masonite is porous, allowing for a strong bond.

◆ Place the rest of the shards, covering all the way to the chair edge.

◆ Fill in all cracks and crevices with grout, especially at the edge. ▶

Finishing Steps

◆ When all the grout work is completed, remove the plastic covering, being careful not to cut the fabric.

◆ Have an upholsterer cover the front of the chair with additional fabric, padding, and piping.

CHUNK CHINA RESTORATION

While working in bits and pieces mosaics, I discovered that many broken pieces I had acquired could be salvaged. There were many great vases and umbrella stands with extraordinary colors and glazes that I couldn't bear to shatter. With a little engineering, I used sculptural elements that seemed complementary to the overall piece to hide the broken areas. In this way, the pieces were restored and saved for many more years of use. In fact, a piece restored in this manner becomes a one-of-a-kind creation.

Base and Materials

Chipped vase, bowl, or vessel

Sculptural elements

Mastic tape

Dremel

Preparing the Base

◆ Find a vase, umbrella stand, or bowl that is broken but still appealing because of its glaze or some other attractive feature you would like to preserve.

Selecting Shards

◆ Choose a sculptural element that complements the base piece. If it does not fit the broken area entirely, additional china, flowers, marbles, or other material can be used to close the gap. ▶

Assembly Tips

◆ You may only be able to glue one element to the base at a time, depending on its weight. Mastic tape can be used to hold heavier pieces until the mastic dries, about eight hours.

◆ When a large sculptural element has a hollow inside, I fill the empty cavity with newspaper soaked in plaster to reinforce the strength of the sculptural piece. Then, I glue it to the base as usual.

Finishing Step

◆ Grind down any sharp edges with a Dremel or file.

Funerary Urn

A funerary urn seems a fitting project for this art form since it preserves mementos from one's life. With land becoming scarce, saving a person's ashes in an urn created with items that have had some importance in the person's life is both practical and meaningful. "Spirit Jugs" or "Memory Vessels" are part of an African American tradition of decorating gravesites with everyday objects thought to be useful in the afterlife. Twentieth-century jugs have been made by a variety of people, reflecting their personal lives and the society in which they lived.

For this urn, which happens to be for me when my time comes, I used as many pieces as possible of the china I have loved, old earrings (including one I wore in high school), coins, crystals, porcelain roses, and more. I have found this a very positive approach to being remembered. When I tease my children that they will have the responsibility of displaying this urn eventually, they tell me that they will be proud to do so.

Preparing the Base

◆ Usually the vase or urn will have a glazed surface that will need to be sanded with coarse sandpaper. Apply a very thin layer of mastic over the entire surface.

Selecting Shards

◆ Collect mementos to use as shards for your funerary urn. Send out requests to family members and friends for tokens to add to the memorabilia you collect for your urn.

Assembly Tip

◆ Make sure the lid on your urn is clear of any shards or sculptural elements and will open and close with ease. Check this function periodically as the shards are applied. ▶

TRANSFORMING JUNK

Miami-born Carlos Alves is an artist who transforms trash into objets d'art. Carlos is, without a doubt, one of the most obsessive and passionate artists working with broken shards and ceramic objects in the *pique assiette* style today.

Carlos has created his own "great wall of china," with piles of dishes that reach some twelve feet to the roof of his studio-storefront on Lincoln Road in Miami's lively South Beach. This collection is an art form itself, plates that are all precariously stacked, waiting for the master to give them an exciting new existence. "Chip it, crack it, smash it. Put it back together and give it a whole new life," says Carlos. He particularly likes to develop architectural applications of broken and recycled ceramics for public places. Some of his creations include murals for train stations, fountains, pools, and hotel interiors.

One project Carlos worked on with Miami Beach High School students was the resurfacing of a nondescript fountain on Lincoln Road. This project was interrupted by Hurricane Andrew, which incidentally produced more broken china for the fountain.

With the help of a grant from Art in Public Places, Carlos designed a mural at the Eighth Street Metromover Station in Miami, Florida, made from recycled ceramics and tiles that had been fused with glass. This mural incorporates ceramic debris collected from the people who live and work near the Eighth Street Station.

Carlos Alves's Ventana Solar (solar window) at the Eighth Street Station serves as a window to the Cuban colonial area of Miami.

CREATING CONTEMPORARY RELICS

There is a growing number of artists working in *pique assiette* around the world today. Some are producing home furnishing pieces for gift shops and galleries, and others are creating art in public places, getting students and other members of the community involved. Many design furnishings, walls, countertops, and floors for restaurants and, in warmer climates, for the exteriors of many public places.

In 1990, Katherine Matheson Kaplan, an award-winning documentary filmmaker and screenwriter, fell in love with the wild shard art. After a few quick technical lessons, she was tiling and grouting anything she could get her hands on. Two years later her husband,

Mitchell, left the restaurant business and joined her in her craft. "Besides making his own beautiful pieces, Mitch is the 'Grout Master,'" says Katherine.

In addition to operating a successful gallery and producing a line of home furnishings they call Relics, Katherine and Mitchell work with designers in preparing displays and restaurant installations. They live and work in an old farmhouse in Warwick, New York, with their daughter, Natalie, and lots of four-legged friends.

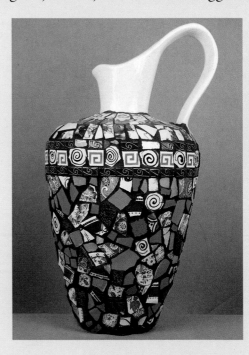

READING LIST

Anscombe, Isabelle. *Omega and After: Bloomsbury and the Decorative Arts.*
New York: Thames & Hudson, 1994.

Beardsley, John. *Gardens of Revelation: Environments by Visionary Artists.*
New York: Abbeville Press, Inc., 1995.

de Sola-Morales, Ignasi. *Gaudí.* New York: Rizzoli International Publications,
Inc., 1984.

Drummond, Allan. *The Willow Pattern Story.* New York: North South Books,
1992.

Fassett, Kaffe. *Glorious Interiors: Needlepoint, Knitting and Decorative Design
Products for Your Home.* Boston: Little, Brown & Co, Inc., 1995.

Isaacs, Jennifer. *Quirky Gardens.* Berkeley: Ten Speed Press, 1995.

Maizels, John. *Raw Creation: Outsider Art and Beyond.* London:
Phaidon/Chronicle Books, 1996.

Rosen, Seymour. *In Celebration of Ourselves.* San Francisco: California Living
Books, 1978.

INDEX

Note: Page numbers in *italic* indicate photos or illustrations.

OTHER STOREY TITLES YOU WILL ENJOY

The Rummager's Handbook: Finding, Buying, Cleaning, Fixing, Using, and Selling Secondhand Treasures, by R.S. McClurg. This handbook for a fun and potentially profitable pastime includes hundreds of tips and advice on finding sales, understanding prices, determining value, bargaining, and taking it home. 160 pages. Paperback. ISBN 0-88266-894-3.

Making Bentwood Trellises, Arbors, Gates, and Fences, by Jim Long. Following the step-by-step instructions in this book by noted landscaper Jim Long, readers will learn how to collect limbs from a wide variety of native trees, then craft and install dozens of trellis, gate, arbor, and fence designs. Full-color photographs of all projects in a real garden setting, and suggestions for vining plants to grow on a trellis or arbor are also included. 144 pages. Paperback. ISBN 1-58017-051-X.

Making Bent Willow Furniture, by Brenda and Brian Cameron. Using the simple instructions and wide range of projects in this book, anyone can make rustic bent willow furnishings for indoors or out. Projects include a quilt ladder, garden tool caddy, plant stand, hanging baskets, chair, loveseat or porch swing, bed headboard, mirror frames, a log cabin planter box, and much more. 144 pages. Paperback. ISBN 1-58017-048-X.

Decorative Stamping: Hundreds of Projects for Your Home, by Sasha Dorey. A step-by-step guide to a popular new way to decorate nearly any surface. 96 pages. Hardcover. ISBN 0-88266-809-9.

Nature Printing with Herbs, Fruits & Flowers, by Laura Donnelly Bethmann. Step-by step instructions for applying paint directly to plants and flowers to press images onto stationery, journals, fabrics, walls, furniture, and more. 96 pages. Hardcover. ISBN 0-88266-929-X.

Making Your Own Paper: An Introduction to Creative Papermaking, by Marianne Saddington. Step-by-step instructions and color illustrations provide the beginner with information about using a mold, pressing and drying, coloring and texturing, preparing a writing surface, and creating paper art and crafts. 96 pages. Paperback. ISBN 0-88266-784-X.

Making Your Own Jewelry: Creative Designs to Make and Wear, by Wendy Haig Milne. Beautiful color illustrations and photos show how to transform beads, semiprecious stones, pearls, crystals, wood, and wire into wearable works of art. 96 pages. Hardcover. ISBN 0-88266-883-8.

Mailboxes: 20 unique step-by-step projects, edited by G.E. Novak. Step-by-step mailbox projects to match any ability, interest, and locale for both post- and house-mounted boxes. 128 pages. Paperback. 0-88266-970-2.

Natural Baskets: Create over 20 unique baskets with materials gathered in gardens, fields, and woods, edited by Maryanne Gillooly. Techniques include waving, twining, coiling, braiding, and stitching of natural materials. 160 pages. Paperback. ISBN 0-88266-793-9.

How to Make Raffia Hats, Bags & Baskets, by Liz Doyle. This book introduces the reader to the basics of working with raffia and provides step-by-step instructions for creating dozens of projects. Dyeing, weaving, and embroidery personalize the projects. 64 pages. Paperback. ISBN 0-88266-887-0.

Be Your Own Home Decorator: Creating the look you love without spending a fortune, by Pauline B. Guntlow. Presented with an infectious can-do attitude and clear step-by-step instructions, this useful book explains how to customize kitchens, living rooms, bedrooms, and baths. Whether a home needs a total overhaul or a 'quick-fix' solution for a problem area, the book provides unique possibilities for beautifying every room. 144 pages. Paperback. ISBN 0-88266-945-1.

Gifts for Herb Lovers: Over 50 Projects to Make and Give, by Betty Oppenheimer. Herb lovers can create herbal body cream, herb-printed notecards, herbal vinegar, an herb drying rack, and much more. 128 pages. Paperback. ISBN 0-88266-983-4.

Gifts for Bird Lovers: Over 50 Projects to Make and Give, by Althea Sexton. Any bird fancier will be thrilled to make or receive these gifts, many of which are seen for sale in popular catalogs and magazines. 128 pages. Paperback. ISBN 0-88266-981-8.

These books and other Storey books are available at your bookstore, farm store, garden center, or directly from Storey Books, Schoolhouse Road, Pownal, Vermont 05261, or by calling 1-800-441-5700. www.storey.com.